Emotionally and Verbally Abusive Relationships

Causes and Effects, Analysis and Solutions

By Larry Tate

Copyright 2015 by Larry Tate.

Published by Make Profits Easy LLC

Profitsdaily123@aol.com

facebook.com/MakeProfitsEasy

Table of Contents

Introduction 5

Chapter 1: The Silent Killer of Self-Worth That Steals Through Our Society 9

Chapter 2: How Conflicting Public Perceptions Compound the Problem 16

Chapter 3: How to Recognize the Emotional and Verbal Abuser 23

Chapter 4: Why Must Abusers Behave so Cruelly? 34

Chapter 5: How Emotionally and Verbally Abused Children are Impacted for Life 39

Chapter 6: The Effect of Emotional and Verbal Abuse on Intimate Relationships 47

Chapter 7: What Happens When Abusers Take over Workplaces? 59

Chapter 8: What Can Be Done to Treat the Emotional and Verbal Abuser? 70

Chapter 9: Solutions for Adults Caught in Abusive Relationships 82

Chapter 10: Solutions for Children Living in Abusive Families 98

Chapter 11: Solutions for Abuse in the Workplace 114

Chapter 12: Emotional and Verbal Abuse in Schools and Higher Educational Institutions . 124

Chapter 13: Elder Abuse: How seniors are victims of emotional and verbal abuse............. 146

Chapter 14: What Happens When the Emotional Abuser is Unstable? 165

Chapter 15: Why We Can't Just Turn the Other Cheek as a Society 182

Conclusion... 192

Introduction

For generations, well-meaning adults have reminded children who are experiencing bullying and name-calling at school to "stay strong and ignore the mean kids".

They repeat the age-old adage that "Sticks and stones will break your bones, but names will never hurt you."

Sadly, it's just not true. Names do hurt. So do insults, demeaning observations and shouting and belittling.

The latest scientific research into the impact of people who suffer from verbal and emotional abuse indicates it is devastating.

Self-esteem is broken. New and often harmful behaviors are formed. Lives are changed forever, and not for the better.

This kind of abuse is often heaped on children, hidden from the trained eyes of social workers and the observations of caring relatives. Because their wounds do not bleed and their scars do not show, the children can endure the trauma until they reach adulthood. By then, they are unable to build sustaining relationships and create the kind of life they deserve.

Emotional and verbal abuse also impacts both women and men in relationships when one partner victimizes the other. Like a thug moving stealthily through the darkness, these abusive behaviors steal their self-esteem and rob them of their chance for happiness and fulfilment in life.

Such abuse also moves into workplaces and institutions. In fact, in any group of people where one assumes power over the others and exercises it with hurtfulness and cruelty of words, the abuse destroys environments and damages those who are exposed to its torture.

Whether because of cultural factors now drawing emotional and verbal abuse into the open or increased awareness on the part of the public and psychologists, instances of this problem appear to be gaining prevalence.

According to the National Coalition Against Domestic Violence, 62 percent of young people between the ages of 11 to 14 say they have already been in a relationship or they know friends who have been in one where they were verbally abused. Boyfriends or girlfriends have wounded their self-esteem by calling them ugly, stupid and worthless.

In this book, the dynamics behind emotionally abusive and verbally abusive relationships will be discussed.

Readers will learn:

- How to recognize the signs of an emotional or verbal abuser
- Why some people express themselves by abusing others
- The impact on children who are verbally and emotionally abused
- The toll abuse takes in an intimate relationship
- The growing problem of abuse in the workplace and what is being done to protect workers
- The prevalence of abuse in educational institutions and what is being done about it
- The emotional and verbal abuse of the elderly in society
- The potential for effective treatment to change abusive behaviors
- Solutions for children and adults caught in abusive relationships
- Handling emotional abuse from narcissists, sociopaths, psychopaths and toxic people

Most importantly, the issue of what is to be done about emotional and verbal abuse will be presented and how cultural, societal and neighborhood attitudes impact attitudes towards this problem.

Chapter 1: The Silent Killer of Self-Worth That Steals Through Our Society

Social workers, psychologists, counselors, teachers and the general public have generally accepted that physical abuse is unacceptable behavior.

Women showing up for work with bruises and black eyes are gently escorted to human resources counselors. Teachers noticing signs of beatings on children are required by law in most countries to contact the police and social workers.

Even though violence is still very much with us, its acceptability as a normal behavior is diminishing.

But there is another kind of abuse that drifts like a ghost in the background of our society, beating people up inside instead of outside. It doesn't show, so some people can't even classify it as abuse at all.

It is emotional and verbal abuse. It is a non-physical expression of violence that threatens the lives and happiness of its victims. Unfortunately, most of them have to suffer in silence.

Emotional and verbal abuse often starts with one person yelling at another person, calling them names and insulting them. The abuser embarrasses the victim in public.

It progresses to escalating stages of abuse, all designed to create a mental prisoner of its victim.

With emotional abuse, if the abuser is a boyfriend or girlfriend or spouse, they may skillfully maneuver their victim away from their support system of family and friends. Isolation is the abuser's desired state for complete domination.

They threaten, they constantly monitor and text their prey, they intimidate them, and sometimes they even stalk them.

Before long, the abuser is telling the victim what to wear and what to eat. They are controlling them even when they are not physically present.

They steal their victim's reputation, spreading rumors about them, threatening to tell their secrets. They threaten harm to the person they are abusing, or they threaten to harm others that the person cares about.

They humiliate them in sexual activities.

In many cases, over time, the emotional abuse escalates to physical abuse.

While physical abuse is an attack on the body, emotional and verbal abuse are attacks on the self.

The victim, watching the essence of who they are and what they do attacked day by day, starts to believe that they are as worthless as their abuser claims. They believe they are stupid and ugly and that nobody else would want anything to do with them. Sometimes they even start to blame themselves for the abuser's horrible behavior towards them.

Verbal abuse frequently begins with name-calling. The abuser can be loud and sneering, like a bully at school, or present their meanness as a form of teasing. In relationships, it continues as insults and unrelenting negativity towards the victim.

It is subtle abuse, even when it is delivered in a roaring voice. Besides a barrage of blaming and accusing and ridiculing, it includes threats, judgments, criticizing, demanding, damning and mocking.

Ironically, verbal abuse can even be silent, as when a person withholds words in a silent treatment as a method of manipulating communication.

People who are yelled at repeatedly often experience symptoms of stress and anxiety.

In an article called "When Words Are Used As Weapons," published on the University of Nebraska – Lincoln Extension website, Kathy Bosch, extension family life specialist writes that verbal abuse takes away a person's self-esteem and impacts their ability to act on their own.

Both emotional and verbal abuse are so destructive because they weaken their victims and leave them drowning in humiliation, hurt and shame. Bosch suggests that this type of abuse can actually be even more demeaning than physical abuse because it leaves its victims more confused.

Physical abuse can be felt and seen. But emotional and verbal abuse are hidden in the shadows of society and move like a fog through the air, impossible to touch or tackle. Sometimes its lack of physical presence makes the victim feel they are imagining it.

Social scientists studying the issue of non-physical abuse have zeroed in on the seriousness of the issue and the difficulty in identifying it in society. In fact, the Conflict Tactics Scale created by Murray Strause that is widely used as a measurement instrument in family violence research deliberately excludes emotions and attitudes in behaviors measured.

But researchers Marisa Beeble, Deborah Bybee, Cris Sullivan and Adrienne Adams at Michigan State University in 2009 noted that there was a particular need for clinicians to address the devastating effects of psychological abuse as they worked with survivors.

In a study called "Main, Mediating, and Moderating Effects of Social Support on the Well-Being of Survivors of Intimate Partner Violence Across Two Years" which was published in the *Journal of Consulting and Clinical Psychology*, they observed the importance of involving survivors of psychological abuse in supportive networks. They found that participating in support groups and group therapy was important for the survivors especially since they had long been separated from their normal support groups in life.

In upcoming chapters, insight on why abusers behave as they do will be presented as well as how individuals and society as a whole can work towards finding solutions to this serious problem.

Studies into why abusers behave as they do will be presented, as well as ideas for the potential rehabilitation of abusers. Most importantly, the actions that can be taken to help victims handle abusive situations and make themselves whole again will be discussed.

At the root of the issue of emotional and verbal abuse is simply one person's desire to control or dominate another. From there, individual motivations become more popular.

In the process, we will show that at some point in time, people all have the capacity to abuse, and we have all be victimized.

If you have ever just rolled your eyes at another person when one person is addressing you, you have performed an emotionally abusive act. If you have mimicked a sibling or mocked them growing up, you have been abusive. If you have enjoyed the laughter that followed from your imitation of a person in authority, you have abused.

In fact, all of these put-downs constitute a form of verbal or emotional abuse.

If you have been on the receiving end of such behaviors in social situations, you likely tried to be a "good sport" and laugh at yourself as others laughed at you, or accept the criticism, however humorously delivered, with graciousness.

Deep down, however, you may have been hurt. At some point in time, all of us have been the target of a joke that left us feeling sad or uneasy. We have listened to a boss blow up and call us irresponsible or idiotic or stupid, and believed we had to take it because it was part of the job. You have been a victim of emotional and verbal abuse.

Victims who complain of hurtful remarks are sometimes told "if you can't stand the heat, stay out of the kitchen," a subtle reminder to victims of abuse to just take it.

What is clear is that nobody deserves to go through life belittled and humiliated. In the coming chapters, we will look at the process of reclaiming the victim's dignity and rebuilding their self-esteem.

Chapter 2: How Conflicting Public Perceptions Compound the Problem

One of the first public acknowledgments of the seriousness of emotional and physical abuse came out of the Women's College Hospital in Toronto, Ontario in 1995.

A study involving 1,000 women over the age of 15 showed that 36 percent had been yelled at or emotionally abused in some way as they grew up. By the time they reached adolescence, the number soared to 43 percent.

In the five years prior to the study, 39 percent of the women said they had experienced emotional abuse in a relationship.

The following year, Health Canada's National Clearinghouse on Family Violence reported that emotional abuse from partners or husbands impacted 39 percent of women living common law or married. Statistics were not gathered for the number of boys and men who had endured emotional abuse from their female partners, even though it is now known that many men are victims of emotional abuse as well.

In general, however, it is extremely difficult to cite statistics about psychological abuse because it is so hard to measure it. Often victims are too ashamed to discuss it, or they lie about it to protect their already fragile self-esteem. Still other times, they refuse to discuss it because they believe they deserve the abuse.

Men who are abused by their wives or female partners are often too embarrassed to complain about it, even to their closest friend or family member. They consider their manhood is at stake and their own ego takes such a daily beating that they cannot possibly bring themselves to endure even more humiliation by talking about it.

Even when children are verbally and emotionally abused, society is confused about what constitutes acceptable parenting skills. Whole generations grew up with threats and being hollered at, and many people still believe that such behavior is quite normal for parents. The theory is that if children are not threatened, they will grow up wild and unable to conform to the manners of society.

If a teacher witnesses a parent being particularly aggressive in words towards a child, they may mention it to authorities, but abuse is hard to prove when there are no physical symptoms.

It is also very hard to prove that a parent called a child a derogatory name if the exchange takes place behind closed doors. And even if it happens in public, the laws of what actually constitutes child abuse are somewhat ambiguous. When a child is obviously being clothed and fed and is not being beaten, authorities often have their hands tied about how far they can push a situation.

Finally, because so many people have been regularly subjected to emotional abuse, they are conflicted on what degree of it is acceptable, and what crosses the line.

Sometimes people accept emotional abuse in relationships with friends just to save the relationship because they still feel it has value to them. For example, a friend coerces another friend to help them move their furniture into a fourth-floor apartment under the threat of telling their girlfriend or boyfriend something about embarrassing behavior they once witnessed. When the job is done, they are all charming and assuring that they would never had said anything, but the victim is not sure.

Sometimes friends manipulate other friends into feeling that they owe them a favor. Other times, a friend will bully another friend into participating in behavior that makes them uncomfortable.

They tell them that if they don't participate they are a prude or no fun or some other verbal insult.

For all the simple conflicts mentioned above, some emotionally abused people have a great deal of confusion over whether what is happening to them in their relationship actually constitutes abuse. That keeps them from reporting it, which compounds society's inability to do something about it.

One of the most comprehensive studies looking at people's perceptions about emotional abuse was published in September, 2014 in the *International Journal of Humanities and Social Science*. Called "Determination of the University Student's Perception of Emotional Abuse," it was the work of two associate professors in Turkey, Hande Sahin and Zeynep Tezel. The study describes emotional abuse by adults towards children as occurring when the adults have expectations that children can complete tasks that are above their skill levels.

Emotional abuse is more prevalent than physical abuse and sexual abuse, they determined.

The university students also perceived that emotional abuse was linked to observations like "my friends underestimate me," "my relatives threaten me to do what they want," and "usually my freedom is restricted," among other things. Yelling at children and teens was considered the most common form of emotional abuse.

A study called "Public Perceptions of Child Abuse and Neglect in Singapore" by Tong Chee Kiong, John N. Elliott and Patricia M.E.H. Ton in 1996 prepared for the Singapore Children's Society revealed that although many people are aware of physical abuse and neglect, they are not familiar with what actually constitutes emotional abuse.

Even in intimate relationships, it can take quite some time before the reality that a partner is an abuser becomes apparent. Emotional abusers don't go through life with convenient labels on their backs to warn others of their disagreeable character traits.

Quite the contrary. Often they are charming and lavishly generous during the dating period. They show up at their quest's office with lunch, spontaneously drop by their house with wine, and cannot do enough thoughtful things. They are almost the perfect boyfriend or girlfriend, manipulating their way into being indispensable.

It is only when the behavior escalates to the point of stalking that their target realizes that what they interpreted as care and concern was really just the abuser's way of checking up on them and making sure they were where they said they were going to be.

Grown-ups who were yelled at and blamed whenever things went wrong as a child often find themselves back living in relationships with partners who yell and blame them when things go wrong. Deep down they are confused. This seems to be a life pattern so perhaps the other person is right; perhaps they are stupid or thoughtless or unable to do even the simplest thing without guidance.

Caught in the dangerous cycle of verbal and emotional abuse, the victim finds it difficult to describe their entrapment, even to a close friend. Every action that is starting to feel threatening could be perceived different by another interpretation. There are so many gray areas that it seems impossible to pinpoint when care and concern turned into smothering and stalking.

If the victim has that much difficulty clearly stating the case of what is happening to them, it is little wonder that society as a whole has such trouble with perceiving what truly constitutes verbal and emotional abuse. When a social problem does not have clear edges, it is difficult to contain it sufficiently for in depth study and to identify specific programs and therapy to deal with it.

Confusion is the enemy of tackling this serious social problem and it will only be through repeated discussion and analysis that courses of action will become clearer.

Fortunately, in numerous academic studies, this elusive issue of emotional abuse is already starting to solidify and therapies for both abuser and victim are being developed.

In Chapter 8, some of the current research into treating the issue will be presented. Meanwhile, it is time to learn more about the abuser and what prompts his or her behavior. By considering both the abuser and the victim with an open mind, a clearer picture emerges.

Chapter 3: How to Recognize the Emotional and Verbal Abuser

Emotional and verbal abusers are walking, talking examples of the old adage that you can't tell a book by its cover.

Both men and women who abuse are often extremely clever, well accomplished, and ooze sincerity and generosity. They charm many who cross their paths in life and draw them close with tremendous personal magnetism. If they are physically beautiful as well, the package is pretty much impossible to resist.

It is only when a person gets close to them that the cleverness is recognized as an extraordinary ability to manipulate, the apparent sincerity is exposed as a mirage, and the generosity transforms to a level of meanness and cruelty that is boundless.

Even as the abuse begins privately behind the closed doors of an intimate relationship, the abuser continues to charm others in a shared circle of friends with the victim to the point that the victim believes they dare not speak of the bad things that are happening. Everyone seems to believe that the victim is lucky to have landed such a "catch."

If the victim does confide in a family member or friend, they are sometimes not even taken seriously. How could such a charmer be so destructive in private? It is unthinkable. Surely there is something wrong with the victim instead that they would say such things.

The abuser knows all about this reality and plays on it to further isolate their victim from those who could support them.

What are the warning signs that a potential new girlfriend or boyfriend is an emotional or verbal abuser? Experts at The Mayo Clinic Health System suggest people pay attention to the following signs when starting a new relationship.

Pay attention when friends of your new partner say that they have "a temper." Notice if they seem to anger easily. Do they seem inordinately angry at the driver in front of them who signals one way and turns another? Are they drumming the wheel while they wait for a slow-moving pedestrian to get out of the crosswalk?

Do they take offense far too easily when you are out with them and other friends? Do they go home fuming over a passing remark that was made early in the evening that nobody else even remembers?

After "temper" comes "jealousy" as a warning sign that the person you are getting close to has some serious controlling issues.

At first, a little jealousy, especially delivered from a charmer, is endearing. A man cannot help by being flattered that his new girlfriend expresses a little jealousy over his ex-girlfriend or some other woman friend with whom he has a close relationship.

Women translate jealousy from new boyfriends as a sign of love and proof that the man really cares for her. When the boyfriend says he wants her all to himself for a day or a weekend, it sounds sweet and romantic. When he complains of always going out with the gang and wants to spend more time alone, it is a signal interpreted in the early stages of falling in love that the other person wants to get to know you better and needs to spend alone time to discover all that is delightful about you.

It is rarely recognized as the beginning of securing total control over your life by creating a gap between you and your support system. If other people are constantly checking on you and caring for you, it makes it harder for the abuser to wield complete control over you.

Another clue is to listen carefully and analyze the kind of stories your new romantic interest tells you. When he or she talks about work, are they always complaining of stupid, incompetent people around them? When a project they are working on fails to be completed, do you hear a long litany of how it would be done now if others had done it their way?

In other aspects of the person's life, are other people largely to blame for any failures to achieve, any impediments to higher education, horrible work conditions, debt loads, and failure to succeed?

If the two of you make a mistake about what time you are to meet or confuse the location or misplace a ticket, is the response that it is always your fault? Even if you know from the start that you are supposed to attend a function at one hotel, and your new partner believes it is another, when he or she is wrong and you are right, is it still turned back as something for which you are responsible? If you had been ready earlier and they'd had time to check the invitation, this wouldn't have happened. If you had not mentioned the wrong hotel first and then corrected yourself, they wouldn't have had the wrong hotel planted in their mind. It may be said jokingly or teasingly, but it is still said. Whatever happens, it is your fault.

Your new loved one, despite their outward charm, seems at first endearingly insecure when the two of you are alone. Even though he or she delivers a speech and earns a thundering ovation, they need to know from you afterwards every single thing that was said at your table. They need to go over and over people's responses and be reassured that they were an amazing success. You feel needed at first, knowing that you are the one person they really trust to let them know what happened. What turns out to be a dangerous lack of self-esteem later at first exhibits itself as a little vulnerability, and it is attractive in its first few appearances.

The emotional and verbal abuser often drinks too much or overdoses on recreational drugs. They become difficult when they are drunk or under the influence of drugs, seeming much more belligerent than when they are sober. Even if they apologize or seem to recognize that a dark side of them came out with too many beers, they still somehow subtly twist it back to you.

"I would have been okay if we had left earlier when I suggested it. But when you wanted to stay for one more round, you pushed me past my limit and that's what happened," they say.

Or they blame it on the crowd you asked them to spend the evening with.

"I don't usually drink too much (or smoke up so much) but your friends are just so boring to me that I had to do something to try to make them look more interesting. You have to admit that they tell the same old stories and they aren't very much fun to be with if you didn't grow up in their neighborhood or work in the same place as them."

When you learn more about the potential abuser you are just getting to know, you often discover that they have a family history of abuse. Even now if you meet their parents you discover that one or both of them makes hurtful comments or insults or humiliates their offspring in front of you. There is hollering and over-reaction to many things. There are guns in the home and threats of physical violence laced into everyday stories.

You start to pick that up in your abuser as well. When a neighbor upsets them, they threaten to go over "and pound them silly." They begin to threaten you physically, perhaps jokingly at first, and then more seriously. "You say that again and you'll feel the back of my hand cross your mouth," or "just wait till I get you home."

They express little patience with children and kick dogs. They express the opinion that many of the problems of the world could be solved with violence.

A characteristic of male abusers is that they have stereotypical views about women. Even though they work with women and may even have a female boss, they embarrass you when they start to talk about women because their views seem from another age. You resolve to change that, but you will fail.

Female abusers, on the other hand, believe that men are inherently stupid and lazy and irresponsible.

Another clue is to check out their past record of relationships. Have they had a fairly stable list of ex-partners, or do they confess that they have had "little luck" in that regard, with most relationships lasting less than a few months? That is a sign that once intimacy or living together occurs, the problems become apparent and people leave them. If your relationship seems to be moving too far too fast, slow it down. It often takes more than six months for the true pattern of abuse to be unveiled.

During sex your new partner likes rape fantasies or other games that leave you helpless.

They experience mood swings, going from loving and tender one minute to insulting and hurtful the next. They are loathe to play up your accomplishments, telling you that you were lucky or just in the right place at the right time.

The abuser at first seems all-caring, always checking on you and showing up unexpectedly. Within a short time, it becomes more apparent that they are checking up on you. They start to accuse you of being unfaithful. They want you to move away with them, quit your job and disengage yourself from your family.

Once you start to live together, they assume control of the finances, even the money that you bring in. They indulge themselves, but insist that you don't need the things you want to buy. Gradually, they control all your spending.

The verbal abuser's behavior is characterized by many of the same things as the emotional abuser. They threaten, they criticize, they insult, they blame, they tease, and they terrorize.

They make demands that those they are abusing cannot possible fulfill. They are manipulative and controlling.

Like the emotional abuser, both men and women can be exhibit tendencies to verbal abuse and both can be victims.

Many verbal abusers also suffer from Narcissistic Personality Disorder or just plain narcissism. Their world revolves totally around them and they expect everyone in their life to serve their needs. Of course nobody can measure up to their standards, so the criticizing and belittling begins.

The narcissistic verbal abuser is totally convinced he or she is the most beautiful and brilliant person in the world, and expresses anger when others cannot meet their all-encompassing need for admiration and control.

In a lay person's terms, we often describe a verbal abuser as "thin-skinned." They become upset at the slightest offense and take to screaming and carrying on at issues other people would simply ignore. To hide their dark self, the verbal abuser will sometimes be extremely charming and attentive, but then change behaviors suddenly, leaving their victims confused and anxious.

The verbal abuser needs to be in charge of virtually every situation. They manipulate circumstances so that they are the only person with the knowledge to solve the problem or make an essential connection. Then they complain about being put upon.

There is no pleasing the emotional or the verbal abuser. They have a perspective on the world around them, and they want everyone to fall in line and reflect exactly what they see. When this does not happen, they turn ugly and the abuse begins. Nobody can speak, think, dress, behave and perform exactly as somebody else wishes, so there will be no reprieve for the person linked up to the psychological abuser.

Both emotional and verbal abusers are natural blackmailers. The charming side of them is able to speedily make connections with new people and they secure secrets that most people will not even confide to their friends. Then they use this information to threaten and control their victims.

If they know their victim has a particular fear or phobia, they will play on it and use it against them.

Another clue that the person you are just dating for the first time is an abuser is their lack of any close friends. They are loners and they will have lots of excuses for that, none of them the truth.

Their only real relationship in life will be with the person who unwittingly marries them and becomes too weak to leave them, so it will be a lie too, like all the others. He or she may claim to be part of "a group" at work, but in reality, they are just on the periphery of real relationships. They have no gang they chum around with, because all their co-workers have written them off.

The verbal abuser never really listens to you or anyone else. Their silence means they are just catching their breath so they can interrupt and correct you.

Finally, one of the most frightening characteristics of the verbal and emotional abuser is that they often morph into the physical abuser.

Chapter 4: Why Must Abusers Behave so Cruelly?

What is it that makes one person believe it is all right to verbally and emotionally abuse another, especially someone they profess to love like their child or their spouse?

There is no quick and easy answer to that question.

In fact, understanding the motivation to abuse others has stymied researchers for generations and it is only in recent years that glimmers of understanding are emerging.

As with physical abusers, emotional and verbal abusers often learn their despicable patterns of behavior from their own parents. Although they may not have been directly abused themselves, they may have witnessed their father abuse their mother or vice versa, and interpreted that as a normal perspective on behavior in relationships.

They may have been abused psychologically at the hands of an older sibling; they may have been severely bullied at school because of a name, an illness, or a physical anomaly, or they may have been reminded of their stupidity and inadequacy from both parents and are still struggling to build their own self-worth by ruining someone else's.

To them, self-worth is a scarce resource; there is not a sufficient enough to go around. If they share it with their partners or children, they believe subconsciously that they will start to suffer again. In the same vein, sometimes they grow up believing that the world has only one rule: be abused or be the abuser, and they decide to save themselves and take the latter role.

One of the most comprehensive studies that looked at emotional and verbal abuse and the characteristics of abusers took place in 2001 at Cambridge University.

Researchers T. E. Moffitt, A. Casi, M. Rutter and P.A. Silva completed research published in the study entitled "Sex differences in antisocial behavior."

They reviewed data collected from the Dunedin Multidisciplinary Health and Development Study done in New Zealand, and concluded that while men are generally considered more aggressive than women, gender was not a defining factor in who would turn into an emotional or verbal abuser.

Instead they identified other common characteristics of psychological abusers.

These included high degrees of jealous behavior and suspicion directed at those they share a relationship with, mood swings that can be very sudden, virtually no self-control, and much higher than average approval rates for violence and aggression in all of society.

Men who are emotional abusers will tackle both the woman they live with and strangers who happen to cross their path, and in both cases unleash a torrent of abuse. Women, however, rarely tackle strangers. They direct all of their emotional and verbal abuse at their husbands or boyfriends.

Besides exhibiting signs of Narcissistic Personality Disorder as mentioned earlier, abusers also have a tendency to show signs of other personality disorders such as antisocial personality disorder and borderline personality disorder.

To put this in perspective, the study showed that personality disorders impact between 15 and 20 percent of the general population. However, 80 percent of the men charged in court with abusive behavior have been diagnosed with personality disorders.

No matter how you describe them, however, the emotional and verbal abuser is a controlling individual. Any kind of abuse still stems from the desperate need of one person to have power and control over another.

Still more insight into the mind and motivations of the abuser emerged from The Duluth Domestic Abuse Intervention Project in 1993 (http://www.duluth-model.org/). At the time, Duluth, Minn. was in the throes of a brutal domestic homicide and the community brought in a group of experts to help them confront the problem of men's violence towards their partners.

In addition to more than the normal number of men being arrested for violence in the home, methods of treatment were sought. With that came the unveiling of new profiles about abusers.

They determined that most of the men who abused believed that it was okay. They received this message through what they had observed or experienced in their culture.

They actually defended their actions with such excuses as "you can't have two captains for one ship or "someone has to be in charge and it might as well be me." They believed that they had a right to use violence to "control" their children, and that it was their responsibility to do so.

Researchers concluded that how both men and women behave in any culture is shaped by the collective experience of the world in which they live. With the abuser, it takes a long time for them to come to terms with the reality that no matter what they have observed, or what is going on around them, ultimately they are responsible for their own actions.

The project also revealed that there was no "one size fits all" description for the abuser. Some were mentally ill, some were narcissistic, and some had no empathy. Many had no remorse for their actions, while some felt ashamed.

Some actually saw themselves as victims of the person they ended up abusing. "I just got fed up with being nagged," they would say. They looked for excuses to justify their behavior, and they found them.

Chapter 5: How Emotionally and Verbally Abused Children are Impacted for Life

Charlie Watson (not his real name) knew he was dumber than a fencepost.

His mother told him so every day for as long as he could remember.

He knew he walked funny, that he was lazy, and he would never amount to anything.

For a long time he walked on eggshells, trying to avoid whatever mysterious ignition system it was that triggered his mother's storms of verbal and emotional abuse.

After a while, he got tired of living in fear, so he built up walls in his head.

He had no friends; who could possibly begin to understand the rotten kind of life he led?

Sometimes he did some work at school, mostly he didn't and there wasn't much the teachers could do to help him. He wasn't letting them past that wall and his mother wasn't the kind of person who showed up for friendly parent/teacher chats.

He missed a grade so now he was taller and even dumber than all the little kids coming up around him.

Sometimes he'd just walk off in the woods and set fire to the insects just to amuse himself. Last week he upped the stakes and burned down old Mr. Burnstill's back shed. He made the fire department come running. He watched from the woods as they all scurried about, trying to keep the flames from spreading in the wind. It was the most fun he'd had ever.

Charlie's life was taking a definite turn and if anyone had noticed, he likely wouldn't be turning back anytime soon.

Charlie, like every child who is emotionally and verbally abused, was trying to heal his mental and emotional wounds. He selected one road, but there are many others.

The reality is that growing up amidst physical and emotional abuse changes a child forever, and for the worse.

A University of New Hampshire study on "Psychological Aggression by American Parents" conducted by Murray A Straus and Carolyn J. Field concluded that despite the popularity of parents using psychological aggression against children to modify their behaviors, it should never be done because of the long-term damage it causes.

When the study was released, angry parents suggested to the researchers that they were implying children would misbehave without such aggression.

However, their research instead showed that avoiding discipline techniques that involve verbal and emotional abuse as well as physical aggression actually increases the probability that the child will be well-behaved and well-adjusted rather than resulting in "kids running wild."

Straus and Field concluded that parents could (and should) criticize unacceptable behavior in their children, but they should do that by criticizing the behavior and not the children as a person.

In this chapter, the impact of verbal and emotional abuse on children will be discussed.

Generally, being attacked with verbal aggression pushes a child to move to one end or another of the aggression scale. Some children become excessively fearful, and that fear cripples them and keeps them a victim for life. They seek extreme dependence in their adult relationships and have a locked-in negative perception of the world. They are over-compliant with their spouses, their friends and their co-workers.

In some cases, this fear manifests itself even in childhood as they experience delayed development. They may resort to rocking, thumb-sucking and bed-wetting behaviors.

Other children, like Charlie as described at the start of this chapter, deal with aggression from their parents by developing aggression within themselves. They become angry and uncooperative and highly rebellious, especially of other authority figures in their lives.

Often the aggression manifests itself in the form of cruelty to animals and setting fires and other acts of destruction.

The aggressive child who sustains emotional and verbal abuse at home turns increasingly towards delinquent behavior. They are extremely passive-aggressive.

Some of their aggression will originally be turned violently on younger siblings and when the child reaches adolescence, they may turn their aggression on their parents.

Once a child adopts aggression as their coping technique, they usually sustain it for life, becoming the verbal and emotional abuser to their own children and their spouse. The multi-generational cycle of emotional and verbal violence continues.

Whether the child becomes extremely passive or extremely aggressive, their reasons are the same. They are suffering from the sustained attack on their sense of self.

Both behaviors indicate that the child is feeling misunderstood and profoundly unimportant. Their self-esteem is undermined and their self-image is extremely negative.

Even if something good happens to them down the road in life, they feel unworthy of it and may mess up opportunities because of their feelings of not deserving anything good to happen to them.

When a child's concept of "self" is destroyed, it is hard for them to even consider growth let alone experience it. They go for decades in survival only mode, still seeking even a shred of worth or value in themselves.

The National Committee for the Prevention of Child Abuse in the United States says such children will often reveal their lack of self-worth by saying things like "I have no friends; nobody likes me," or "I am too stupid to do that."

Children who are withdrawn, depressed and sullen are all exhibiting symptoms of low self-esteem.

Sometimes they will go so far as to perform self-destructive acts such as cutting their wrists with razor blades in an expression of their own loathing for themselves. They will carelessly place themselves in danger because in their deepest heart, they cannot really perceive themselves as being a person worth saving.

There is no age at which children seem more able to handle verbal and emotional abuse than others. For example, an infant who is fed and changed, but who receives no nurturing or expressions of love and caring and is spoken of negatively from the start, will fail to bond with his or her mother. They do not move ahead on the same physical and mental growth as other babies. In fact, doctors have a name for these babies. They describe them as "failing to thrive." In extreme circumstances, these babies will even die.

If the child does survive and grow, often they become extremely insecure and anxious. Even as the years pass, they still are unable to thrive.

They become consumed in the throes of depression and severe anxiety. In short, they grow physically, but their spirit is broken.

They are prone to self-destructive acts.

Besides the developmental and psychological issues that develop in the verbally and emotionally abused children, there is a raft of social and relationship problems inherited as well.

They drift further into anti-social behavior and withdraw from the world as a normal child lives it. Going back to the New Hampshire study, children were found to express their inability to build relationships with negativity. Sometimes they hit other children, or they picked fights with their classmates.

It is the beginning of a life-long estrangement from social relationships. Their relationships are often inappropriate or troubled. They lack empathy and are unable to understand or meet the emotional needs of their spouses or children.

It is hard for them to be happy in a relationship because they have built a wall around their true emotions and have never really understood the concept of trust.

Oftentimes, they just give up, unable to function in society at all.

A perspective on how the abused child becomes increasingly antisocial is featured in the scientific study "A developmental perspective on antisocial behavior" by G.R. Patterson, B. D. DeBaryshe and E. Ramsey.

Many youngsters who are verbally and emotionally abused drift into alcohol or drug abuse and slip away from their futile quest for any kind of emotional bond in real life.

Not only are they socially crippled, but intellectually, they bear the scars of verbal and emotional abuse as well. Such children's academic skills are often impacted. Their creativity is locked, and they are unable to access their cognitive ability.

Compounding the problem of helping the child who is the victim of emotional and verbal abuse is the difficulty in detecting it. While physical abuse can be detected by its scars and marks, the child abused with words suffers undetected in silence.

Chapter 6: The Effect of Emotional and Verbal Abuse on Intimate Relationships

Earlier in this book we answered the questions of why abusers behave as they do and the impact of their actions on their weakest victims, their children.

This chapter deals with another perplexing question about the entire issue of emotional and verbal abuse. That is, why do the victims of abuse take it? Why don't they leave bad relationships? Why don't they stand up for themselves?

Like so many other questions about human behaviors, the answers are complex and still unfolding. In this chapter, the impact of emotional and verbal abuse on the person who takes it, day in and day out, sometimes for a lifetime will be discussed.

What happens to victims of emotional and verbal abuse from their spouses over time? And why do they stay living with the person who treats them so badly?

As strange as it may sound, sometimes the victims think what is happening to them is just a normal way for people to interact. They may have been victims of the same kind of abuse (or combined with physical abuse) when they were children, and when they marry a person who continues to abuse them, they assume that is normal. In a bizarre way, they are not actually aware that they are being abused. They think that's the way people are.

Other times they know the difference, but they fail to run for fear, for lack of financial or emotional resources or because their self-esteem finally gets so broken they lack the stamina to try to put it together again.

They are so demeaned that they lack the ability to set boundaries on what they will accept and shattered in spirit, they surrender control of their own life to someone who will take it and waste it.

It's easy to think clearly and plan get-away strategies from a distance, but to the person who is taking the abuse regularly, the perspective is never clear. From their cloudy, mentally-beaten up point of view, they fall into a maze of possibilities and just can't find the way to the highway. Sometimes they can no longer even find the road to what is acceptable and not acceptable, so they live their lives in limbo, knowing what they have isn't good, but never understanding how it could be better.

Adults who accept verbal and emotional abuse have their own set of common characteristics, just as their abusers do.

As a general rule, they tend to have a low sense of self-worth. They are anxious and insecure. In fact, that tendency makes them vulnerable to the strength of their abuser in the first place. They are often looking for someone who will "take care of" them.

They have submissive personalities and often believe that they deserve the bad way they are being treated. They feel inferior and not as bright as the people around them.

Many victims have never achieved financial independence or the lifestyle skills to be emotionally independent. In looking for protection, they are vulnerable to those who would take advantage of their weakness and exploit it for their own needs.

The emotionally abused spouse does understand periodically that they are not being treated right. They may fear and even hate their abuser. Often they start to build and live in an imaginary world where everything is better. In their darkest moments they have dreams that someday things will suddenly change and it will all be okay again. Perhaps they will be whisked away by a knight in shining armor. Perhaps their spouse will just die and leave them with all their money and a good-looking and nice replacement spouse will beat a path to their door.

Friends of emotional and verbal abuse victims often describe them as "too" tolerant. They are the people content to just go along with the wishes of the crowd. Whatever somebody else wants to do is fine with them.

When people in their lives have problems, they consider that it could be their fault. In other instances, they blame bad luck or the world in general, or the dark side of life, of which they see a lot. They tend to be negative in their perspective of the world.

They can't say "no" easily and believe that as bad as their situation is, at least they have a roof over their heads. They can't even imagine how they could make it alone in the world. At the same time, they do not see a link between their own personal weakness and the way they are treated by their abuser. Frequently deluded, they don't even see it as abuse, just "moods" their partners go through.

When it's over, they maybe given a crumb of affection and they will gulp it eagerly, satisfied and hopeful again that things will be better soon.

It is this decision of the victim's to put up with things, that maybe they are not so bad after all, that frustrates those who are willing to help them.

The long-term danger to the victim is that they never grow to become what they could be in life. They never set their own destiny or dream their own dreams. They shiver in fear in the background of somebody else's life, thinking it still might be better than stepping alone into the sunlight.

Depression sets in. At some point the abuse victim recognizes that life is passing by and they have achieved nothing. In extreme cases, they may be driven to suicide, believing the world would be better off without them and that they have absolutely nothing to live for.

Though their characteristics add up to the suggestion that the victim is weak and even a bit to blame for living the life they do, nothing could be further from the truth.

One of the reasons their self-esteem prohibits them from running and living their own life to the fullest is that it becomes, over time, absolutely destroyed by the manipulative words and actions of the verbal and emotional abuser. Their lives and their spirit is being broken, day by day, one insult and humiliation at a time.

By the time others become aware, sometimes they are too far down the self-esteem pool to swim to the surface again.

Before the victim of emotional and verbal abuse can truly receive help openly, they must first be convinced that what has happened to them is not their fault.

It is not their fault that their partner suffers from certain mental health disorders or was scarred by his or her childhood. It is not their fault that they got mixed up with such a person and then became too broken in spirit to help themselves. It is not their fault that they did not recognize from the beginning that the pattern of behavior could never lead to a healthy relationship.

That's a vitally important aspect of helping the abuser, according to the National Network to End Domestic Violence.

They tell women victims in particular that they can't be blamed for hooking up with the wrong guy. They missed the signs because their new boyfriend was very smooth and generous and caring. How were they to know what he was really like?

The National Coalition Against Domestic Violence suggests that about 85 percent of the victims of all kinds of violence in the home are women. One out of every four women will be abused either emotionally, physically or sexually, and rarely will they ever report it to anyone.

Meanwhile the Center for Relationship Abuse Awareness pegs verbal and emotional abuse as one of the most serious issues in society today and one of the least understood.

When women find themselves receiving such abuse, the impact is almost immediate and it can last for life.

For example, the woman starts to doubt her instincts for spontaneity and her enthusiasm for life and fun diminishes. She becomes very uncertain about how other people perceive her and starts to worry that there is something wrong with her.

She spends time going over and over events that have happened, trying to figure out where she went wrong. As her self-doubt grows, her self-confidence diminishes.

Sometimes she even develops an inner critic who tries to second guess what is wrong with everything she is thinking. She begins to think she is going crazy. She has the vague notice that her life is passing and she is missing it, but she doesn't trust herself enough at this point to believe her own thoughts and perceptions.

She wants to escape from her life and run away, but she is afraid and lacking the resources. She doesn't know where to run to or what she could do.

She begins to dream of a better future where there will be a happy ending and everything will be okay. The worse it gets, the more she dreams.

If she does escape, she is often scarred for life. She is fearful of new relationships, never wanting to return to the dark side of emotional and verbal abuse, never sure she can trust the new person in her life who is promising, as before, to love her and take care of her.

While there is a lot more research available on the impact of emotional and verbal abuse in an intimate relationship on women, there is a growing interest in studying the impact on men. It has traditionally been difficult to gather data since abused men suffer further from a society that can laugh at their problem or think they are less of a man because they have allowed the abuse to happen.

Men who are emotionally and verbally abuse often develop difficulty in making decisions and coming to conclusions. They are waiting for their wives or girlfriends to tell them what they should be thinking and doing. The pattern is so engrained that often they will not even make decisions on insignificant things like what kind of bread to buy or what kind of movie they will see.

Men suffering sustained psychological abuse believe even more intensely than women that there is something definitely wrong with them. Deep down, they are convinced that they are too sensitive or too selfish or even just crazy.

Like women, they go over and over encounters to try to figure out where they made their mistakes and how they could have had the same encounter and secured a different outcome. They become afraid to communicate, for fear that they will say the wrong thing and unleash a tirade of abuse.

They too start to lose their spontaneity and enthusiasm for life. They self-doubt rises and their self-confidence sinks.

They believe that things will magically get better if certain other circumstances change. It will be better if they buy a new house, go on a vacation, have a baby, or make other life changes, but instead, it only gets worse.

Over the long term both men and women often develop physical symptoms because of their prolonged exposure to stress and anxiety. Migraines and other frequent headaches, chronic pain, ulcers, digestive disorders including diarrhea and spastic colon and stress-related cardiovascular disease can be linked to verbal and emotional abuse.

There are mental as well as the physical consequences.

Both male and female adults experience sometimes crippling fear and stress, post traumatic stress disorder, memory gap disorders, hyper-vigilance and exaggerated startle responses, anger issues, alcohol and drug abuse, sleeping and eating disorders, self-mutilation and sometimes suicide.

Diane England, author of *The Post-Traumatic Stress Disorder Relationship* and several articles on abuse, addictions and narcissism, believes that people who endure emotional and verbal abuse for years even suffer an impact in their brain.

She points out that our hippocampus, part of the limbic system or "emotional brain," controls most of the involuntary aspects of emotional behavior that are related to survival. It also dictates how we respond to emotions such as fear and anger as well as happy emotions like love.

If a person lives in a toxic environment where they are subjected to emotional and verbal abuse over a long period of time, the hippocampus can start to atrophy. The result, detected through magnetic resonance imaging, is stress-related disorders like depression, PTSD, and Cushing's disease. Stress also paralyses the production of new neurons. If that is not bad enough, it even impacts the memory, making it difficult for the victim to place things in context.

Even though PTSD is most commonly associated with soldiers returning from combat where they faced extreme stress, it is also a byproduct of years of verbal and emotional abuse. This further weakens the victim, leaving them even more helpless to the whims of their abuser. The adult victim of psychological abuse is actually brain-washed over time to accept that they must do as ordered, without question.

At the University of South Australia's School of Social Work and Social Policy, Associate Professor Dale Bagshaw goes a step further in discussing the impact of emotional abuse on adults. He suggests that the long-term effects can be just as devastating, if not more so, than the impact of physical violence.

His remarks were based on the Australian component of the International Violence Against Women Survey that found about 40 percent of women reported experiencing controlling behavior in some format.

In a follow-up article, Bagshaw suggested that other people's words affect how we see and feel about ourselves. When the words are negative, full of complaints and criticism, they tear away at the recipient's self-image. Attacks on our self-image leave marks just as surely as bruises and wounds, but they take longer to be visible.

The long-term impact of verbal and emotional abuse on both children and adults is serious and lasting. But the confines of family are not the only avenues for such abuse. Many people experience it on the job as well as the next chapter will explain.

Chapter 7: What Happens When Abusers Take over Workplaces?

One of the most complicated forms of verbal and emotional abuse occurs in the workplace.

It comes from two sources: co-workers and bosses.

The complication is that it is an unwieldy behavior for companies to get any control over. Unlike sexual harassment and physical assault, obnoxious and abusive behavior is technically not illegal unless threats and feelings of being unsafe are involved. The abuser often has to deal with it alone or accept it, even though some companies have become more sensitized to the issue in recent years.

Still, in some business cultures, having a boss who curses and shouts and threatens workers is actually considered the norm. Workers who complain are reminded by their boss's boss, who has the same attitude, that they are lucky to have a job and "if you can't stand the heat, stay out of the kitchen."

Emotional and verbal abuse from a direct supervisor is more damaging to the worker in the long run because the worker feels like he or she just has to take it. If they challenge the boss and try to stick up for themselves, they risk worse abuse or being fired for insubordination or given an increasing load of the worst possible tasks.

Examples of workplace verbal and emotional abuse include yelling, swearing, threatening, insulting, mocking and teasing workers either in private or in front of their colleagues. It can include inappropriate jokes or compliments of too intimate a nature, vicious gossip, insinuations and ridicule.

Dr. Loraleigh Keashley, associate professor and Master's Program director at Wayne State University, Detroit, and Dr. Steve Harvey of Williams School of Business and Economics at Bishop's University in Quebec, in a study called "Workplace Emotional Abuse," reported that about 24 per cent of the American workforce reports being emotionally abused repeatedly over a long period of time. This often involves a hostile relationship with bosses.

They described the incidents these workers were experiencing as creating a psychological work environment akin to being under siege. Operating like that for months and even years takes a high toll on workers as well as the other people in their lives, like families and friends, who try to support them through their ordeal.

The abused worker sustains a number of psychological effects ranging from anxiety and negative moods to depression, alcohol and drug abuse, fear of increased violence, and cognitive distraction.

Prolonged exposure to emotional and verbal abuse in the workplace can make the victim respond with their own form of hostile aggression or passive aggressive resistance. Sometimes the victim experiences hyper vigilance and emotional exhaustion. The byproducts of those states include poor job performance and accidents.

The continuing state of abuse at work spreads to the support system of the worker, and family and friends become co-victims, picking up on the fear of their loved one losing their job and source of income and coping with the upset and negativity of the victim.

When workers become paralyzed with fear and respond with their own form of resistance, it does not work well for the organization either. The cost in increased stress leave, accidents, and failure to complete tasks competently rises.

In a 2003 study, "By any other name: American perspectives on workplace bullying," Keashley and Jagatic discovered that unlike relationship abuse, in which men are the more common abusers, in a workplace males and females engage in emotionally abusive behavior at about the same rate.

In 2011, researchers Hslang-Chu Pai and Sheuan Lee discovered that younger workers were most at risk, largely because of their lack of job experience and their inability to identify or avoid potentially abusive situations. Their study, "Risk Factors for Workplace Violence in Clinical Registered Nurses in Taiwan," was published in the Journal of Clinical Nursing.

The same study showed that 51.4 percent of the nurses surveyed had already experienced verbal abuse. Almost 30 per cent of them had experienced bullying and mobbing within the workplace.

There is a difference between having a conflict with a co-worker and experiencing abuse from them. In any work environment there are people who do not like each other but are forced to work together for economic survival. Being cold and stand-offish, for example, may be annoying traits in a co-worker, but they are not abusive. If that co-worker suggests every day that you are too stupid to understand the work at hand, however, that is abusive.

When a co-worker or a group of co-workers signals out a person for bullying, he or she can emotionally zoom right back to the school hallway. Nothing has changed; the bullying is just done by older people in work clothes. The victim will feel hurt, anxious and perhaps even fearful that they will not be able to survive in that environment.

If a boss insults a worker, threatens them with dismissal or demotion, reminds them regularly how lucky they are to have a job with their limited abilities, or unleashes tirades of anger about their performance when they least expect it, the situation becomes even more serious.

The effect of working in such a situation can leave victims full of anxiety and affect their mental and physical health over the long term. They may start to doubt themselves and experience diminished self-confidence and self-esteem. They may start to think that they could not get another job and that they are trapped in this one.

They become afraid to take a day off, and if they do, their thoughts anxiously turn to their work many times throughout the day. They are embarrassed to take the abuse, but feel helpless to stop it. They start to lose their capacity for fun and spontaneity. They feel alone, unable to confide in people for fear that they will think their boss is right.

Over time the impact of the abuse grows. In some cases it is similar to brainwashing. As the bullying boss manipulates the victim's emotions, they become confused to the point that they no longer recognize which feelings are their own and which ones are their bosses. Bit by bit, day by day, their sense of who they are, their sense of self, is eroded.

Workplace bullies, like schoolyard bullies, tend to target people they assess as weak in some way. They are observant of the people around them in their own way, and able to attack when their actions will have the most devastating effects.

In *The Bully-Free Workplace*, authors Dr. Gary Namie and Ruth Namie observe that bullies will pounce abusively on heart attack victims the first day they return to work, on new mothers the first day their maternity leave ends, and on cancer sufferers the first day they return to work after their chemotherapy starts. They are ruthless.

The result of such cruelty in the workplace is that millions of men and women all over the world hate going to work. Their mental and physical health suffers. Some end up quitting a job to which their skills and aptitude are best suited and taking under-employment as they try to mend their broken spirits.

The Namies suggest that nearly 14 million adults in the United States work in circumstances where they are bullied and endure other forms of emotional abuse. They believe that business has to take the issue far more seriously, since it is preventing work from being completed and costing them millions.

The theme of underlying costs of emotional abuse to companies and institutions was also a focus of a study called "Disruptive Behaviors in Healthcare: Implications for Patients" completed by Lynn Lenz and R. Krajewski at the University of Wisconsin, La Crosse in 2009.

They noted that emotional abuse in a health care environment can occur when staff members release their anger and frustration on coworkers. The result is impeded communication and eroded teamwork which leads to avoidable medical errors and the risk of malpractice. It also compromises the quality care that patients expect from their health care system.

Because of the life and death risks that result, they urged immediate action on tackling the issue.

The term "mobbing" often arises in connection with workplace abuse. Swedish psychologist Dr Heinz Leymann, who conducted research on issues relating to workplace hostility in the 1980s, described mobbing as a kind of "psychological terror."

The worker's colleagues or superiors attack their dignity, their competence and their integrity repeatedly, often going as far as to even accuse them falsely of wrongdoing. Humiliation is a daily occurrence.

Leymann listed 45 mobbing behaviors that included constant criticism, withholding information, badmouthing, circulating unfounded rumors, isolation, ridicule and yelling.

Mobbing differs somewhat from bullying because in mobbing, there is an indication that it is not one person against one person, but rather a "gang" abusing one person. The gang leader can identify the target and summon his or her troops to action to make that person's work life miserable. Shockingly, mobbing is often management driven, so the victim has no recourse but to take it or leave.

Mobbing is one of the most psychologically damaging forms of workplace abuse. Nobody is safe from it. It crosses all barriers of gender, age, race and physical characteristics. The strong and vibrant young man can be the victim just as easily as the weak and older worker in a wheelchair.

It is interesting that in the book *Violence at Work* published by the International Labor Office (ILO) in 1998, mobbing and bullying are classified on the same list as rape, robbery and homicide. The authors explain their reasoning is that while these two forms of violence may seem less harmful than others, the effects on the victim can be devastating to the point that they end up committing suicide.

Still other victims have reacted in an explosion of extreme violence on their own part, commonly referred to now in our culture as "going postal," taking other lives and their own in a dramatic finish to punctuate that they can't take it anymore.

In many instances, being the victim of mobbing and bullying at work leads to nervous breakdowns, sleep disorders, panic attacks and heart attacks. It impairs the victim's ability to concentrate and seriously affects their job performance. Extended sick leaves often result.

When the attacks make it impossible for the victims to perform their jobs capably, often they are the ones terminated, leaving a blot on their employment records, while their tormentors get off free and clear and ready to tackle their next victim.

Even after leaving the violent environment, emotionally abused workers can suffer from post-traumatic stress disorder.

The seriousness of the issue has led a number of companies and researchers to try to figure out how emotional and verbal abuse starts in the workplace. What triggers it?

The ILO determined that the source is often an unresolved conflict that escalates to an extreme point far in excess of the original issue at stake. This prompts them to remind companies to put policies for conflict resolution in place.

How is it that such a serious problem can continue, unchecked, in so many workplaces around the world?

One reason is that emotional and verbal abuse is either ignored by managers or encouraged as part of their strategy.

Another is that many companies have no policies or means of addressing it, and thus just leave it alone as something they will have to deal with down the road, but just not now.

Finally, there has been an absence of lawsuits launched by victims, largely because by the time they exit the company, they are too emotionally beat up to take on another fight of that proportion. But there are signs that is changing as well with the growth of zero-tolerance for harassment behavior in the workplace.

Chapter 8: What Can Be Done to Treat the Emotional and Verbal Abuser?

Can an emotional abuser change?

That is the question that has confounded therapists and psychologists on many levels for many years.

One school of thought is that they can change. The reasoning is that abuse is a behavior the abuser learned, and as such, it can be unlearned or readjusted to a more acceptable behavior.

The other school of thought is that the particular qualities of an emotional abuser are such that they render most therapy ineffective. They will lie, manipulate and even charm their way through it, promising change, and then promptly revert to their old habits.

The story of the emotional abuser and the therapist, they suggest, is like the old Aesop Fable about the scorpion and the frog.

The scorpion and the frog meet on the bank of a stream and the scorpion asks the frog to carry him across on its back. The frog asks, "How do I know you won't sting me?" The scorpion says, "Because if I do, I will die too."

The frog is satisfied, and they set out, but in midstream, the scorpion stings the frog. The frog feels the onset of paralysis and starts to sink, knowing they both will drown, but has just enough time to gasp "why?"

Replies the scorpion: "It's my nature."

Is it the nature of emotional abusers to continue their ways all through their lives? Will they lie and make false promises and then, even though they are hurting themselves as much as their victims, continue to abuse?

In this chapter that question will be considered against a review of approaches to treatment for the abuser and the potential for their success or failure.

If there is one overall conclusion consistent through all the literature, it is that for any program of therapy or intervention to be successful in changing the abuser's behavior, they must commit to it totally.

They must agree to stay with the program and follow every step on the road to change.

They must also agree that they have a problem and they want to solve it.

If they are dishonest about that essential step one, then they will not succeed. If they agree to take a program but secretly believe they have no problem, the process will be a total waste of time for all involved.

Most of the therapeutic approaches to changing an abuser's behavior focus on educating the abusers on how to express their anger or disappointment in different ways, rather than belittling and humiliating and screaming at people.

In further stages, it tackles their propensity for controlling behavior and helps them to understand the impact of their actions.

Treatment programs, often adapted from those used for physical abusers, tend to take the framework of consciousness-raising exercises. They focus first on helping the abuser and the victim create a vision of an abuse-free relationship. The next stage is the teaching of new communication skills, and the third stage is discussing problems that will likely occur. The final stage is a positive affirmation of the changes that have occurred.

Most of the people who are convinced to take treatment as emotional and verbal abusers have problems believing that they are abusers. They think that as long as they do not lay a hand on the other person, they are not abusers. They are unaware and often uncaring of the internal, emotional scars they are leaving on their victims.

The abuser in therapy will often express worry that their partner will leave them and is motivated to keep them dependent.

Dr. Phil, the popular television psychologist, addresses questions on his website that every abuser, emotional or physical, should consider. He wants them to think about how their actions really impact their partner. He preaches that respect is commanded, not demanded. Abusing someone is not constructive, he suggests, and it will not create the wanted results.

Dr. Phil urges abusers to realize they don't have to behave badly and to apologize to those they have hurt.

The American Psychological Association, in an article entitled "Can therapy help an abuser," says statistically, the odds are against effectively changing an abuser.

However, there are certain characteristics that do indicate a sincerity for change in the abuser who seeks treatment. They have to admit they are abusive and that their behavior is their fault, not someone else's. They have to want change and be aware that the process of change is hard. They have to participate in an abuse assessment process with a professional who specializes in such things, and they have to be willing to do what that professional recommends.

They have to enter programs voluntarily to address their specific abuse issues and commit between four months to a year to regular attendance. Finally, just as an addict accepts that even though their problem is under control, it still lurks below the surface forever, so must the abuser accept that while they have stopped abusing, their tendency to emotional and verbal abuse will remain with them for life.

If they can meet all of those specifications, they can change the way they behave and return to normal, healthy relationships with their spouses, their children and their co-workers.

Promises to do better after flair-ups are empty if they are not linked to the actions and attitudes mentioned above.

The experts at the American Psychological Association also counsel that abusers who are also narcissists or psychopaths will not benefit from the treatment programs.

Most people know someone who has been sent on anger management courses or sensitivity training and are aware that within a short time, they return to their former loathsome behavior. One of the reasons a lot of those programs fail is that they are about educating the abuser about the victim's point of view and building empathy for the victim; But if the abuser is a narcissist, they may be incapable of understanding or experiencing empathy.

In these programs the abusers are also guided to examine the source of their anger and behavior, but abusers do not all function or react like each other. In some cases they do become more aware of their motivations; in others, they do not.

The APA suggests that each abuser actually needs psychotherapy customized to their individual needs. They should be tested to see if they suffer from Borderline Personality Disorder or Narcissistic Personality Disorder.

Additionally, many abusers also suffer from substance abuse which must be addressed before their larger issues of unacceptable behavior can be tackled. Abusers should also be checked for brain damage.

Abusers who accept that they are abusers and want to change have to overcome the misconception that in certain circumstances, their behavior is acceptable. There are no circumstances in which it is okay to humiliate, control, and insult others.

They must then seek help from professionals to learn new parenting skills, new interpersonal skills and new ways of expressing their frustration and anger.

The field of research into finding successful therapies to treat emotional abusers is a broad one as health professionals continue on their quest to solve this serious social issue.

A new Florida State University study has implications for a different approach to treatment, for example.

The study, co-authored by Natalie Sachs-Ericsson and FSU psychology Professor Thomas Joiner, was published in the *Journal of Affective Disorders*. Researchers from the University of Illinois at Urbana-Champaign and the University of North Carolina at Chapel Hill also participated in the comprehensive project that looked at data from 5,614 people aged 15 to 24.

The researchers discovered that people who sustained verbal abuse as children had 1.6 times more symptoms of anxiety and depression as those who did not. They were also doubly likely to suffer mood disorders or anxiety disorders in their lifetime. They were much more self-critical than people who were not abused as children.

The study has impact in how abusers might be treated. Earlier research showed that people suffering from self-criticism can be helped with cognitive-behavior therapy. In that, the participants begin to recognize their irrational thought patterns and replace them with rational thoughts. They are also taught new behaviors to help them feel more at ease in uncomfortable situations, the kind of circumstances that would normally make them lash out.

How can you tell if your verbal or emotional abuser suffers from self-criticism sustained by the poor parenting skills of their own mothers and fathers? In tests, they will answer in the affirmative to statements like: "I dwell on my mistakes more than I should," or "There is considerable difference between how I am now and how I would like to be."

Children who were physically or sexually abused growing up also had more self-critical attitudes than those who did not.

Marcia Stanton, a social worker coordinating child abuse prevention efforts at the Phoenix Children's Hospital, is one health professional who has taken to the Internet to urge continuing research and attention to the issue of children who are emotionally abused themselves turning into abusers.

In an article called "How Early Experiences Impact Your Emotional and Physical Health as an Adult", she said why, if we can immunize children against illnesses like chicken pox, can we not find a way to immunize them to the larger threat of growing up in an abusive environment?

Commenting on the Adverse Childhood Experiences (ACE) Study prompted by Dr. Vincent Felliti in the 1980s, Stanton said it is clear that time does not heal the wounds of childhood.

If ways cannot be found to intervene and treat abusers and protect the children, the trauma will continue, she suggests.

Finding the courage to leave an emotional or verbal abuser is sometimes the spark that causes them to seek help. But many victims who leave are lured back by promises of change, and they return, only to find that nothing at all has changed, except that their self-esteem is lower than ever.

Many emotional abusers are adept at creating cycles of being abusive and cycles of being thoughtful, constantly keeping their victims off guard. But even when they are in their good cycle and apologize for the hurtful things they said earlier, the damage has already been done. The self-esteem of the victim is irreparably harmed.

However, one expert in the field of emotional and verbal abuse who still believes some abusers can change is Lundy Bancroft, author of *Why Does He Do That? Inside the Minds of Angry and Controlling Men* and the former co-director of Emerge, a pioneer program for abusive men.

He writes that in his extensive practice, he has seen some abusers dig deep within themselves and identify the values that make them abuse others. Once they are aware, they find the strength to create new ways to interact with their partners.

But even when this happens, the change is difficult and demanding work. The abuser, once he or she searches deep enough to understand why they are doing it, must be able to continue looking in that dark place for a long, uncomfortable period of time.

Like the victims they humiliate and belittle, they too have serious self-esteem issues and they have to find whole new ways to build themselves up without reaching out and bringing others down.

There are many approaches offered to help abusers change behaviors. Some show modest successes, and some actually seem to make things worse.

Sometimes a family member or authority figure will force an abuser and their spouse into couple's therapy or individual therapy. While well-meaning at the time, it can actually make things worse.

Meeting a therapist with their spouse present, the abuser can be extremely adept at misrepresenting the situation. Remember, they were clever enough to persuade someone to marry them. They turn on the charm and can even have the therapist believing that they are actually the victim, trying desperately to placate an unstable partner.

In summary, to get better the verbal and emotional abuser has to accept who they are and what they do. Their behavior is often rooted in self-preservation. They blame others to shore up their own inadequacies and are totally able to justify their actions as essential for their survival. When they begin to understand where their behaviors came from, they may be able to make constructive changes.

Chapter 9: Solutions for Adults Caught in Abusive Relationships

There are a number of different theories about how best to deal with an emotionally abusive relationship as an adult, but all of them focus on the bottom line that the victim cannot let it go on, or he or she will never recover wholly and restore a sense of self.

It is not easy to counsel someone on what to do when they have many complicated issues to consider. If the emotional or verbal abuser is their spouse and they have children together, there is more of a motivation to try to fix the relationship than if it is casual and break-up is more of an option.

In this chapter, the latest research on the subject of "what to do" will be presented as options for the person who is experiencing abuse on a regular basis.

In many, many cases, especially when the abuser suffers from Narcissistic Personality Disorder or Borderline Personality Disorder or other conditions that make change unlikely, they have to consider ending the relationship as quickly as possible.

Steps must be taken to secure their safety and the safety of their children during this process.

If the relationship is uncomplicated, particularly if there are no children involved, then the victim can just leave. If the victim is not living with the abuser, they can just break up. Stop seeing the person who is emotionally or verbally abusive abruptly. Do not hesitate, do not think that they can be changed or fixed with more love. The victim should just cut their losses, chalk it up to experience and get out of the relationship.

If the abuser pursues the victim, the latter must take immediate steps to cut them off from their life completely. The victim must avoid going to any of the places where they know they are likely to encounter the abuser, even if it means upsetting their own social life temporarily.

Victims are counseled to take the following steps:

Change the locks on your house or apartment if your abuser had a key, or ever borrowed yours (they likely made a copy). If there is a doorman at your apartment, show them a picture of your abuser and ask them to notify you if he or she turns up looking for you.

Change your computer and banking passwords. Take the time to change your passwords for social media as well, because a common tactic of the emotional abuser is to resort to humiliating you on line when you try to end the relationship.

If your relationship with the abuser is more complicated, as in the case of marriage and/or children, you will have to prepare yourself to leave and then follow through. If the emotional abuse has at any time escalated to physical abuse, it will only get worse. Go now while you can.

When you live with a controlling emotional abuser, it is extremely challenging to find any time to yourself to make your plan of action. As soon as they notice you doing anything different in your routine, they will challenge you and demand explanations.

That is why the time from making your decision to leave and getting out has to be very short. The essentials you need are a safe place to stay, a way of getting there, and a sufficient pocket of time to escape safely. It is also a good idea to have contacted or secured the information to contact a lawyer who can represent you from this point forward in any dealings with your abuser, if you have shared property or are married.

If the abuse hasn't escalated to a physical stage and you can endure the emotional abuse long enough to open a separate bank account and slip some money into it, that is a great idea. Of course, the problem is that many emotional abusers ensure that you are financially dependent on them, so this may not be possible.

If you can get the bank account, make sure you have a private post office box where any documents can be sent. Controlling abusers check all the mail and may even be roaming through your computer files when you are out of the house.

If there is no opportunity to do this, see if you have a family member or a friend who will agree in advance to help you for a short period of time to get back on your feet. Ask them for a loan (you can agree to pay them back with interest) just to help you purchase groceries and essentials until you can secure employment and live independently.

Some domestic violence agencies also recommend that you hide a packed overnight bag so you can leave at the first available opportunity. Of course, the danger here is that your abuser will find it. It is difficult to find safe hiding places in the average house or apartment.

It is a better idea to just start keeping your overnight toiletries in a plastic bag, to keep a couple of changes of clothing neatly folded in a drawer with a plastic bag under them where they will not attract undue attention. Make a habit of keeping your prescription medicine in the corner of the same drawer. Keep all your essential pieces of personal identification in one purse always kept in one place, right on top of that bureau. If you have a passport and your abuser has not already taken it from you, keep that with you as well.

When you are able to escape, you just have to grab the bag from your bathroom, the bag from your dresser drawer, and your purse and throw them into a duffel bag. You may also have a computer, an iPad, a phone and other personal devices. Start now to keep them all in the same case for the same reason. Make it part of your established routine to put your iPad by your purse or in it, for example.

If you keep a daily agenda for work or family appointments, create a simple code to document extreme outbursts of abuse. If you have children and will be filing for custody of them, this can be used in court.

One woman created a system where "m.e.a.l planning" meant "must escape after lunch" and referred to her new resolve after a torrent of abuse was unleashed on her. Looking back over a six-month period, (during which time her spouse kept promising to reform and then returned to his old ways), she noticed that it was occurring more often, and crafted her genuine escape plan.

"Clean fridge" meant her spouse blew up over means or household matters, "finish work" meant he went ballistic about the fact she had to work overtime.

When she finally left, she spent a few hours the first week she was gone writing up the instances of abuse, explaining her code system, and presenting the whole documentation to her lawyer, keeping a copy for herself.

If you have a phone that has a recording device, or a small recorder that can be used to record one of your abuser's verbal tirades, that is also a useful way to establish your case for custody. If the tirade includes threats to you and your children, it can be used to launch a legal investigation as well.

Always keep in mind that when your abuser is confronted by a social worker or a court judge, they will be doing their best to undermine you and make you appear emotionally or mentally unstable. They will be composed, even charming, and extremely manipulative. Your word alone may not be enough to make your case that this person is not fit to raise your children.

Throughout the process of escape, as difficult as it is, you must always keep in mind that it is not your fault what has happened. You did nothing to earn this kind of treatment. You deserve to live in peace. There is nothing you can do to placate an abuser or make them love you again as they appeared to during your courtship. That ship has sailed.

Make every effort you can think of to keep your abuser out of your life or from encountering you in any way. Change grocery stores; ask a colleague to accompany you to your car or bus stop after work until it is clear that you are not being stalked.

If your ex-spouse or ex-boyfriend or girlfriend starts to follow you, keeps hounding your friends for details of your whereabouts, calls you repeatedly, sends you unwanted letters or emails, shows up at your workplace or at your door, and leaves you unwanted gifts, you are being stalked.

Experts at The Stalking Resource Center of the National Center for Victims of Crime say stalking is a frightening experience and makes you feel anxious and depressed, even after you have summoned the courage to leave an emotionally abusive relationship. It can impact your ability to move on with your life, cause sleeping and eating disruptions, and affect your ability to concentrate on your work.

Seek help if the person keeps stalking you. Tell the police and outline the threats this person has made to you in the past. If you feel in danger, go to a domestic violence shelter or the police station, or to a friend's house or public area. Call 911 if you are in immediate danger.

Secure a restraining order against your stalker, requiring them to avoid all contact with you.

As with the incidents of emotional and verbal abuse, keep a record of all incidents when the person has followed you or contacted you. Take photos of them at your door or in your workplace, and print and date them. Secure names of witnesses. Confide your problem to your employer, your landlord, and your family, neighbors and friends. Keep a cellphone with you at all times.

Add motion sensitive lights to the exterior of your house and secure locks.

As adults remove themselves from emotionally and verbally abusive situations, they are particularly vulnerable to new relationships where they are promised protection from their past abuser.

It is important to remember that this is one characteristic that attracted you to your abuser in the first place and not rush into a new relationship with a controlling person and falling into the same cycle again.

You cannot move too fast to enter a new relationship, because you need time to heal. You will recover, and you will be ready, but not immediately. You need to restore your sense of self-worth, to understand who you are and what you are seeking in a relationship, before you go out and fall into the same situation as before.

There is a huge danger of victims of emotional abuse self-sabotaging themselves by falling again for the same kind of person.

However, given time, you will be able to more clearly assess new relationships and pick up warning signs that you missed previously. You deserve love and respect, and you will find a partner who delivers that, but you need to give yourself room to recover first.

Many victims of abuse find it useful to attend meetings of a domestic violence support group.

It helps them to talk freely about their experience in a room full of people who truly understand. You learn from each other as you progress back to a feeling of self-reliability.

These groups will help you understand deep-down that what happened is not something that you did. It will lighten your burdens of guilt and anger and regain your perspective on yourself and on life. Most of all, it will put you back in touch with that most powerful of all emotions, hope.

At the same time that you are examining the past, it is important to leave time to take specific actions to move you into the future. Take on a new hobby or some volunteer work. Explore a new interest or make an effort to get your body fit along with your mind. Try to work a little fun back into your life.

You may start by reading books and enjoying television shows, but make sure some of your new relaxation involves engaging in social activity with others. Relax with people you love and trust. Rebuild the gap that occurred when you were an emotional prisoner of your abuser. Do creative things, like taking an art or dance class, learning to play a musical instrument or taking a night course in cooking or carpentry.

Start directing your conversation to stories about these new activities when friends and co-workers ask you how you are. You do not want to be labeled a victim the rest of your life. Show them by your stories that you are recovering and engaging in life again.

Some victims of abuse find it helpful to move on with life by getting a pet. A little dog that you have to go out and walk, who is waiting delightedly for you to get home, and who curls up with you can be a great comfort in restoring your understanding that you are worthy of love and attention. You might step into pet ownership gradually, first by offering to keep a friend or neighbor's pet while they are away to make sure that you can handle the commitment, and moving forward from there.

In *Love Without Hurt: Turn Your Resentful, Angry or Emotionally Abusive Relationship Into a Compassionate Loving One*, Dr. Steven Stosney, founder of Compassion Power in Washington, D.C., says it is important in recovering from emotional abuse to ultimately find compassion for yourself and for the other person.

Stosney reminds readers that we all know someone who has experienced emotional abuse at some point of their lives. He believes that the problem is actually getting worse because we have created a culture where people believe they are entitled to feel happy.

When they don't feel happy, they imagine that someone is taking it away from them, that their rights have been violated, and they turn on the person closest to them. They are hostile and angry at the world, but they express it to the person they have the most chance of controlling.

Just as the victim of emotional abuse feels their chance of happiness is being taken from them, so does the abuser. They feel resentment to a world that has not delivered on its promises and powerless to change it. So they move to secure power within their own small domain, their home.

In the same vein as Stosny advocates compassion, other experts in the field of domestic abuse advocate healing as a means to complete recovery.

Kelly McDaniel, who wrote Ready to Heal, says people recovering from emotional abuse constantly remind others that the relationship wasn't always the way it ended.

To keep them from falling for the same kind of person again, she writes that they must learn to put their own well-being ahead of everyone else's. That is much more difficult than it sounds for the person who is burdened with guilt, a beaten self-esteem, and remorse over the failure of a relationship.

People have to understand that they cannot be responsible for someone else's happiness. We can only choose to be happy ourselves. Learning that is part of the healing process.

The abuser must accept that same reality if they are to recover and change.

If you blame the unhappiness you feel on your partner, you will never take the steps to address it yourself. If you hurt, your brain is sending you an alarm. You need to change your circumstances; you need to correct what is wrong, or take steps to improve on what you are doing that is not working now.

Happiness comes from being able to live your life in sync with your values. Take time as you recover from emotional and verbal abuse to get in touch with your value system again and consider how life would look if it were lived in accordance with them.

Dwelling on your past relationships will not help you adjust to finding happiness in the future. It is only when you figure out the kind of life that you want to lead that you are ready to engage in a relationship with someone you believe will be a suitable partner in that life.

We have looked at leaving and healing as options to dealing with emotional abuse. What happens to the person who, for whatever reason, chooses to stay in the relationship? Can anything be done to survive this and retain any sense of self-worth?

Again, through assembling all of the information from domestic violence centers and scientific studies into the nature of abuser and victim, there are some steps that can be taken to protect yourself if you live with an emotional abuser.

It is important to find the courage to start sending the message that the abusive behavior is not okay. For the verbal abuser, when the yelling starts, it is time to quietly get up and leave.

Leaving sends an eloquent message that the behavior that is happening is not acceptable. It reminds the victim that they are still in charge of themselves. As in leaving for good, you need a plan of where you can go for at least a night.

If your emotional abuser turns physically violent, call for help.

What you should not do when an outburst is in progress is to apologize or try to reason with the person who is yelling at you. Standing your ground and defending yourself may be possible in some situations in life, but this is not one of them. The emotional abuser will not see reason at this time.

A common response of the abuser is to resolve that they will not listen to the tirade, that they will put up an emotional wall and not let the person hurt them anymore. Sadly, they cannot do that over any period of time with any degree of success. They may think that they don't hear and it is not impacting them, but it is seeping through that wall and slowly tearing away at their self-esteem.

Victims should not make excuses for their spouse if an outburst takes place in front of friends, or if they are humiliated and demeaned in their presence. They must remember always that it is not your fault. Their behavior is not something the victim caused, and they are not responsible for it, nor can they control it.

If the friend brings up the subject the next day when the spouse is not around, the victim should not say their spouse was just over-tired or had one glass of beer too many. Instead, they should say calmly and quietly that their spouse was verbally abusive and they are hopeful things can be worked out, because they cannot endure such behavior repeatedly.

Much of the literature available on what the victim of emotional and verbal abuse should do is directed towards women. But unlike physical abuse, in psychological abuse, the victim is just as likely to be a man as a woman.

The abused male victim suffers from the same attacks on their self-esteem and they start to doubt themselves and believe they are somehow responsible for the unhappiness of their abusive female partner. They keep hoping that she is just having a mood of some kind and that things will be better and she will be more loving if he can just hold things together for a while longer. Sadly, as with male abusers, the situation does not change except to get worse.

Chapter 10: Solutions for Children Living in Abusive Families

More than 20 years ago, a telephone survey revealed that by the time a child reached two years of age in America, they had been exposed to one or more forms of psychological aggression by their families.

Dr. Steven W. Kairys and Dr. Charles Johnson, in a study called "The Psychological Maltreatment of Children" published in the *Journal of the American Academy of Pediatrics*, discovered that psychological aggression, which they described as controlling or correcting behavior that caused a child psychological pain, was more prevalent than corporal punishment such as spanking.

In the same study, they discovered that 10 to 20 percent of toddlers and half of all teenagers experience severe aggression from their parents.

Such behavior included threatening to send the child away, belittling the child by calling them stupid or dumb and cursing at them.

What can be done to help children who are exposed to such verbal and emotional abuse?

Kairys and Johnson were of the opinion that pediatricians have a role to play in educating parents to understand that children who grow up without supportive and loving words can be greatly harmed. Pediatricians can also reinforce to parents that children need to be loved consistently, regardless of their behaviors, they must be accepted and they must receive considerable attention.

On a broader level in the community, the doctors suggested that home visitation by experienced health professionals can be successful in helping parents at risk of psychological abuse of changing their approach. Programs that target mothers with behavioral disorders and substance abuse issues have experienced some success.

The organization Prevent Child Abuse America says dealing with the issue of emotional and verbal abuse has always been challenging because it is harder to identify and diagnose.

Professional clinicians do sometimes use an adapted form of the Child Abuse and Trauma Scale (CATS). It provides a kind of system of measurement of degrees of emotional abuse.

Babysitters and day care workers can also help by watching children's actions and personalities carefully. Caregivers can also closely observe children's behaviors and personalities. Children who are being emotionally abused are often extremely close to their parents and very loyal. This is not necessarily love; it can be they are afraid of being yelled at if they do not. They learn to think that how they live is normal.

Signs to check for are if the child seems either less mature or more mature than his or her colleagues of the same age. Watch for changes in behavior like seeking affection in the extreme or disrupting activities, bedwetting, being uncooperative and destructive behavior (bullying other children) or antisocial behavior (being sad, withdrawing from other children).

Watch for the child who has difficulty making friends, is very unsure of themselves, and has unusual fears of some objects or of being left alone, even for a few seconds.

Although caregivers may suspect emotional or verbal abuse, they have to watch the child interact with his or her parents to get a better idea of what has happen. If the emotional abuse is coupled with signs of physical abuse, the caregiver has protocols to report it and an investigation is launched. Without physical abuse, it is more difficult to move in to protect the child.

Educational materials can be made available to all parents, so as not to signal out the suspect one. Free seminars could be offered to encourage good parenting skills.

The issue of what to do has challenged experts in the field for more than 50 years.

Many psychologists believe emotional abuse falls into a kind of gray area that is difficult to get a handle on. As far back as 1988, leading child abuse researcher Deborah Daro was noting that public intervention in cases of emotional abuse is limited, even though there is substantial proof that this kind of abuse seriously affects a child's development and ability to function socially.

The work of researchers Giarretto (1978) and Dale et al (1986) indicate very little focus has been put on how to assist youngsters from recovering from emotional abuse. "Woefully inadequate" is the way Melton and Thompson described the situation in 1987.

Today there is a growing school of thought that general family support programs can be helpful in making parents aware that they should not yell at or threaten their children.

The idea was pioneered in 1987 by B. Egeland and M.F. Erickson in a study called

"Psychologically unavailable caregiving: The effects on development of young children and the implications for intervention." They suggested a model for intervening with high-risk parents to help them better understand their children, including having realistic ideas about normal behavior and aspects of childhood development. The idea of supporting high risk parents in times of extreme stress and crisis was also presented.

In 1995, A. Fortin and C. Chamberland wrote of their study called "Preventing the psychological maltreatment of children" in the *Journal of Interpersonal Violence*. They suggested a four-part approach to tacking the issue. It included easing socio-environmental stress, reducing dysfunction in families, promoting parenting skills and parent's self-image, and offering social support.

That same year, McCluskey and Millar came out with the idea of theme-focused family therapy dealing with nothing but the inner-emotional world of the family. At the crux of their therapy was a strategy to slow the pace of talk between family members, providing time for reflection before speech. They also advocated giving children a chance to speak throughout the process of family therapy.

A Canadian researcher, Dr. David A. Wolfe of the University of Toronto and author of the book *Child Abuse: Implications for Child Development and Psychopathology*, took another approach. He suggested a solution could be approached from the angle of tackling the development differences that come from the child who is being maltreated and which impact their ability to learn normal social behaviors.

As opposed to just working with parents, he suggested working with the children directly to show them new methods to structure their experiences and help them develop the socio and emotional skills to form relationships. He believed this could be done by helping to build up the child's sense of self-identity and self-differential. The key to accomplishing this was through better child-parent relationships or extra-familiar opportunities.

Wolfe also tried to move away from the idea of the parent as the bad person in the relationship and look at their needs and try to fill them by showing them effective parenting methods that would work better for them and their children in the long run.

Others built on that idea, suggesting it was not useful to see abusive parents as an evil stereotype. More could be accomplished, suggested researchers Wilczynski & Sinclair in 1996, by addressing more underlying causes of emotional abuse such as lack of parental support and poverty.

But the cycle of people being abused as children turning into parents who abuse their own children emotionally and verbally continues.

Meanwhile, throughout the world a number of knowledge communities tried to tackle the issues of the emotional abuse of children.

In the United States, for example, the National Committee to Prevent Child Abuse came out of Chicago with a campaign that said: "Children believe what their parents tell them. Watch what you say. Stop using words that hurt. Start using words that help."

Australia came out with a similar campaign called "Use Words That Help Not Hurt" which their National Association for the Prevention of Child Abuse and Neglect came out with. It expanded over the years to a National Child Protection week theme of "Let's Talk with Children," which focused on positive ways adults could communicate with little ones. A "Healthy Families Project" that took place in the schools also gained popularity. It stressed a positive approach, and advised children they have the power to change their lives and urged parents to treat their children differently than how they were raised if they were emotionally abused themselves.

In Canada, the Nobody's Perfect program educated parents of children from birth to age five.

In 1998, two developmental psychologists named Michael Lynch and Dante Cicchetti suggested the problem could be approached from four levels of interaction.

Their process, labeled an "ecological transactional analysis" and published in the journal *Development and Psychopathology*, cited these four factors as impacting on emotional abuse in children:

- The macrosystem: includes cultural beliefs and values that permeate society and family functions
- The exosystem: includes neighborhoods and community settings which families and children live
- The microsystem: includes the family environment in which adults and children create and experience

- The Ontogentic development: includes the individual child and his or her own developmental adaptation

Lynch and Cicchetti developed the idea that each and every one of these zones contains risk factors that expose a child to verbal and emotional abuse. Any approach that focused only on one area and ignored the others, for example, would be ineffective.

In other words, psychologically abusing children is not just a matter of dealing with the parents. It is dealing with a community that is not in judgment of them for doing so.

In practical terms, if you have recognized yourself as an emotionally or verbally abusive parent, what steps can you take to change? Or, if you are just starting out as a new parent, and you were emotionally or verbally abused yourself, how can you help from passing on the cycle of mistreatment?

The American Humane Association reminds parents to never be afraid to say they're sorry to their children. If they have yelled at them in the past, called them names, implied that they were stupid, they should start the process of change by apologizing for saying those things in anger, and tell them they simply aren't true.

They offered a number of other ideas to parents who were trying to change their abusive behavior.

From this point forward, make every effort not to call your child names when you are displeased with their actions. When you use words like "good for nothing" and "lazy" and "dumb" and "ugly as sin," you are wounding them and leaving a scar that will never heal.

Understand that your child deserves respect, just as surely as they must have food to eat and shelter from the cold. Even if your child behaves in a way that displeases you, you can express displeasure over the behavior, but not over the child.

When you feel anger building and you want to lash out and scream, let that rush trigger a return to calmness instead. Ask the child to take a "time out." This will give you time to get over the heat of the moment and think more calmly how to deal with inappropriate behavior.

When you have calmly considered an appropriate punishment for bad behavior, tell the child what they did wrong and that they have to make amends and not do it again.

Find opportunities to praise your child for the good things he or she does. Even if it is just a little behavior change, like taking his dirty dishes to the sink, comment on it and say you appreciate the help.

If you feel you are losing control of your temper, be sure to walk away from the situation until you regain control. Decisions made in the heat of the moment can have long-term consequences on the physical and mental health of your child.

If you feel like you are experiencing frequent outbursts of anger, as if almost everything the child does incites you, try to figure out what is really happening.

The American Academy of Pediatrics suggests you try to understand the reasons why you are so upset.

You may feel like your children are suddenly trying a lot of new things that are troublesome and you want to stop this trend, but you don't know the ways to communicate these concerns to your child. They may have a new group of friends that you feel are a bad influence, but you cannot find the way to express your observations to them in a respectful way.

You may believe that verbal abuse, especially threats, are necessary for the child's good. You see it as tough love, but in reality, love isn't tough. You have to find other ways to talk about what is happening with them.

You may find it impossible to control your own strong emotions like anger. There are proven techniques available, through books, articles, group therapy and private therapy to help you learn how to keep a lid on your volatility.

If you were emotionally and verbally abused by your own parents, be conscious that you are predisposed to pass on this parenting style to your own child. Remember how it felt and how you reacted. Is this how you want your child to feel about you?

Meanwhile, the next time you experience the wave of anger rising within you, try to stop it by calming your breathing. Take deep, slow breaths, inhaling and exhaling to still the turmoil inside you. Wait until you are calm before you address the child.

Deal only with the misbehavior that has occurred at this moment, not things that happened yesterday or last week.

Try to think how your child is feeling when they see how angry their behavior has made you.

Take a different approach to what has happened. Try using humor.

Listen to what your child tells you and hear the whole story.

Parents are not the only ones who can help lessen the psychological impact of emotionally abused children. In cases where children have not suffered long term damage from emotional abuse from their parents, they have consistently had someone else in their lives who gave them support and shored up their self-esteem.

When you suspect that a child is suffering from emotional abuse, you can befriend that child, especially if you are a teacher or a church leader, a day care worker or anyone who has close and direct contact with them.

Reassure them of their value and their intellect. Help them achieve things.

In a study by researchers Woodham & Lapsley in New Zealand in 1996, children who had been emotionally and verbally abused but who had managed to avoid serious psychological impact spoke fondly of their saviors. These were supportive people who were there for the children when they began to doubt themselves.

These people helped the child to feel they were worthy and that they could make good decisions and figure out for themselves what was right and wrong. Because they had this outlet, they were also able to better detach themselves emotionally from their parents and not be as affected by their parents' words.

Just as parents may not be the only ones who can reduce the impact of emotionally abusive behavior on a child, neither are they always the perpetrators of the abuse.

Many children are abused in school, by babysitters, by church or community leaders, and by others who have authority over them.

As a parent, be mindful of the changes in your child that could signal something has changed in their lives. Whenever possible, meet their teachers, their coaches, their music teachers, and all the people who will spend time alone with your child. You will likely already be checking their references, but check other parents whose children have taken lessons or training from these people.

If your child starts to suddenly hate guitar lessons, even though they enjoyed it for two years before, find out if a new teacher who is verbally or emotionally abusive could be behind their reluctance to go.

Listen to what your child says about teachers when he or she is talking with friends. If you get hints that the children are being humiliated or threatened, check further into the situation. Make a point of talking with your child and getting them to repeat what is said to them about their performance.

Children will sometimes be reluctant to talk about verbal or emotional abuse because they are too ashamed or humiliated, or because they don't recognize it as abuse. So watch for other behaviors, especially reluctance to go certain places, as signs that something is wrong.

What happens if you encounter a parent verbally or emotionally abusing their child in a public place?

Authorities advise that caution is better than valor if you are thinking of confronting the parent. Chances are you will make them even angrier and more abusive and the child will bear the brunt of it when you turn away.

What you can do is take the subtle approach of diverting their attention. Even a bit of empathy can help. For example, let's say a child pulls at a display in a supermarket and several oranges tumble to the floor. The parent is yelling at the child for doing that. Instead of telling the parent to stop yelling, just bend down and help picking up the oranges and say something like "my six year old once knocked over a table that was full of pies." I laugh about it now but I remember how it felt."

Chapter 11: Solutions for Abuse in the Workplace

When the United States Workforce Bullying Institute released a report in 2010 that revealed a shocking 35 percent of workers said they were bullied on the job, the nation expressed dismay.

Some thought the number was high in these days when worker's rights are supposedly protected through legal statutes and unions. But experts in the field of emotional and verbal abuse in the workplace suspected the number was actually a little low. Many people are loathe to admit that they have been humiliated and verbally abused on the job, feeling it makes them look weak and unable to handle themselves.

Of the types of workplace abuse described in the report, verbal abuse rated tops.

Dr. Harvey Hornstein, author of the book *Brutal Bosses and Their Prey*, figures that workplace abuse is nearly an epidemic. He suggests as many as 20 million Americans daily walk into workplaces where they are yelled at, humiliated and disrespected.

For many workers, it is difficult to fight back. Their verbal abuser is most frequently their supervisor or someone who has authority over them. Some of these bosses just lack the management skills to handle the jobs they are in, and they resort to the only kind of behavior they know to get their point across.

Some are narcissistic and believe that it is the job of everyone around them to serve them, and they can't understand even the slightest resistance.

Others believe they are running some kind of boot camp, where it is their job to break down the defenses of their employees and see what they are really made of. They take delight in their toughness, lashing out at those who cannot fight back. These same people can be charming and manipulative to their bosses to the point that complaints about them are dismissed out of hand as lacking credibility.

Next to verbal abuse, mobbing has become a most serious form of emotional abuse in the workplace. As explained earlier, mobbing happens when a group of co-workers target a person in an effort to break them and get them to leave. While the social and dollar impact of mobbing hasn't been measured yet in the U.S. economy, it is increasingly recognized as a growing issue.

The victim of a mobbing suffers deeply and some have been driven to suicide.

In the book *Mobbing: Emotional Abuse in the American Workplace*, authors Noa Davenport, Ruth Schwartz and Gail Elliott say that mobbing starts when the worker is targeted for disrespectful and harmful behavior. Through innuendo and rumors spread by their co-workers, they are forced to deal with an increasingly hostile work environment until they break or leave.

Mobbing most often happens in businesses where production areas are poorly supervised or management is especially inattentive to their duties. Sadly for the state of the corporation, the person most often treated with such emotional abuse is the one who works harder, faster, more intelligently or more creatively than those around them. They are also usually more honest and dedicated to the company.

Mobbing will continue in workplaces all over the world as long as it is permitted to happen by incompetent and inattentive managers.

Companies that pay no attention to civility and ethics are breeding such behavior.

In recent years, however, the problem of all kinds of verbal and emotional abuse in the workplace is getting more public attention and both management organizations and academic researchers in the field of workplace dynamics are turning their attention to what can be done about it.

If you are targeted for mobbing in your workplace, what can you do?

Just as with any victim of emotional abuse, the first step is to understand fully that it is not your fault. You did not do something that unleashed the dark side of your co-workers. They are the ones behaving badly, not you.

Consider what will work best for you under the circumstances. Is there someone who would listen to you within the management ranks? Do you have a union representative who is not part of the mobbing crowd?

Are you in a situation where you can just cut your losses and find another job? Can you transfer within your company to another department? Do you need any further skills or academic qualifications to make the move? Can you endure the abuse long enough to acquire them?

For your own long-term physical and mental health, you need to realize what is happening, acknowledge that it is abuse, and determine a course of action to follow. You must take control of your handling of the situation, or it will color your workplace relations for a lifetime.

Try not to show signs of weakness, the standard response to dealing with bullies since schoolyard days. But if you are experiencing physical and mental health symptoms that could have serious long-term effects, you need to get out of that atmosphere as quickly as you can.

Do you qualify for stress leave? By seeking help for yourself, you will trigger a reaction within the company that something is horribly wrong in the department where you work.

Chronicle specific instances of abuse; tape some comments if you can. Save any derogatory emails you are sent or notes that might be left on your desk or in your locker.

You should see your supervisor as a matter of course, or your human resources department. If they take your complaint seriously, they may tell your abuser to stop, and that may solve the problem. On the other hand, the bullying may get worse.

If your supervisor does nothing about your problem, you may have legal recourse against the company in the long run, but you will have to be able to show a pattern of emotional abuse existed. If you speak to a supervisor and nothing is done, document the date and time of your meeting, if there were witnesses, and anything else that would be convincing to prove the meeting took place. Send a follow-up email to the supervisor you spoke with, thanking them for their time and briefly summing up the topic of discussion. Print that email if you can, or at least ensure that there is a copy kept on your home computer. If you have to leave suddenly and all your documentation is on a work computer, it may be taken as you exit and you will have nothing.

Managers have a responsibility to ensure a safe and respectful work environment for all employees. If a lawsuit follows the claim of an employee who says they were terrorized and threatened on the job, the manager who failed to see the problem becomes just as guilty as the perpetrators of the mobbing.

All companies in this modern age need to have written policies that specify the respectful treatment expected for all employees, and that policy needs to be posted and followed. Civility in the workplace needs to be a common practice.

In the United States, the right to work safely and without threats in a healthy workplace is protected by law, although the words "verbal abuse protection" are not used. However, the federal Occupational Safety and Health Act (OSHA) provides for businesses to be liable if employees are not safe. Employers can be held responsible for allowing an abuser to carry out outrageous behavior directed at their employees.

In 2008, for example, the Indiana Supreme Court awarded $325,000 to a nurse for her claims of intentional infliction of emotional distress and assault after she was screamed at by a surgeon.

In several European countries such as Germany and Scandinavia, new safety laws cover aspects of the emotional health and safety of employees on the job.

An example is the Swedish National Board of Occupational Safety and Health's adoption of an Ordinance Concerning Victimization at Work. This was passed in 1993.

In Australia, telephone hot lines have been created for victims of mobbing and emotional abuse on the job and addresses for therapists who can help in these situations are widely circulated through newspapers.

If you are suffering abuse at work and you feel strong enough to confront the abuser directly, make sure you do it by the book. Tell the abuser clearly that you will not continue to be subjected to their emotional abuse. Rather than go into a litany of accusations, tell the abusers it is not so much what they are doing as the effect it is having on you.

If they respond with more abuse, advise them that the behavior that has just occurred is an example of what you find is troubling. Tell them that if they continue to abuse you in this fashion, you will have no alternative but to report them to a supervisor.

Chances are your abuser will respond with more abuse. At that point pull out the corporate policy or human resources handbook and make them aware of the section under which you will be reporting them. This will help when you have to go to the supervisor and are asked to print up an account of the conversation.

Any company that does not currently have a policy against bullying and emotional abuse should have. The policy should have zero tolerance for emotional abuse and stress the standard of respect expected within the workplace. Examples of what constitutes verbal or emotional abuse should be explicit. A protocol for making complaints should be created to protect the victims.

Print and distribute the policy to all employees and have it framed and posted in each department. Ensure that each employee reads the policy and signs a sheet signifying they have read and understood it.

Policies are nothing but pieces of paper if they are not enforced. Ensure that a protocol is also set in place to handle any complaint with consistency and professionalism.

Businesses that must deal with the public also occasionally must deal with customers or clients who behave in an emotionally or verbally abusive manner.

While police officers, flight attendants, teachers, and even retail and customer service employees are the most likely to be emotionally or verbally abused, it can happen in any business that deals with the public.

In recent years in particular employer responses to complaints of threats to employees.

In 2012, the Society for Human Resources Management released a Workplace Violence Survey that indicated 47 per cent of companies fire an employee who threatens another. Twenty-nine per cent would suspend the employee for a certain amount of time and 31 percent said the employee would be given a written warning.

Employers also said they immediately became more vigilant about enforcing their anti-abuse policies after a complaint is filed. Hidden cameras are often placed on production lines, extra security lights are added and closed circuit television systems are installed.

Human resources departments are instructed to do more comprehensive character checks on new employees and to conduct tests that bring out aspects of the personality of managers. They are also asked to train managers and supervisors how to detect signs of verbal and emotional abuse.

Chapter 12: Emotional and Verbal Abuse in Schools and Higher Educational Institutions

The changing face of emotional and verbal abuse within education facilities has become increasingly evident since the advent of widespread use of social media.

At Canada's Dalhousie University in Halifax, Nova Scotia, for example, there are still legal ramifications stemming from a Facebook page that was created in the first few weeks of the 2011 semester.

Some of the early posts were apparently harmless, but within a few days the content became aimed at female students on the campus's dental school and became what one follower later termed as sexually violent.

The subject is still in the news since the ramifications are continuing both in public courts and behind the closed doors of the university's administration.

The site had 13 members who called their site Class of DDS 2015 Gentlemen on Facebook group. All of them have been now ordered to attend classes apart from the regular class and are suspended from clinical duties, which could affect their ability to graduate.

Meanwhile, the university has announced they will appoint a task force to look into what happened and a restorative justice process will hear from those involved. And the story is still in headlines since a lawyer for one of the Facebook members says they were pushed into accepting the punishment without due diligence and a proper investigation by the university to identify which members were actually active on the site.

The women who complained saw the Facebook page as just another form of emotional abuse.

It takes the idea of psychological abuse within educational facilities to a new level and the ramifications are still being discussed in other facilities around the world.

In a totally different vein, but still in the field of emotional abuse in schools, the no-zero policy of schools in Newfoundland and Labrador on Canada's east coast was rescinded in 2015.

No zero policies became popular in many Canadian schools in recent years. The idea was originally to separate the behavior of a child from their academic achievement, just as parents are reminded to separate the behavior of their children from an attack on the child themselves.

Proponents argue that teachers, in an effort to separate the behavior from the child's achievement, should not correct bad behavior such as cheating on tests, handing in late work and refusing to pass in assignments with an academic mark of zero that will affect the student's long-term grading average. The proponents say teachers should find other ways to deal with the bad behavior.

The reality of that theory in schools where it was implemented proved that it only served as a catalyst to create even worse behavior. Knowing they could not be given a zero, students became increasing lax about due dates. Teachers felt they were left without enforcement options.

Gradually, the no-zero policies disappeared from most Canadian schools.

These two unrelated stories signal the different approaches education facilities are struggling with as they try to find appropriate ways to teach children and have them conform to school rules, without resorting to threats and emotional abuse. They are signals that authorities are looking for new, thoughtful ways to deal with the issue, and that is encouraging.

Sadly, however, for many children, their first experience with being emotionally or verbally abused still occurs in the classroom.

In a 1997 study called "Emotional Abuse: The Hidden Form of Maltreatment" by Adam M. Tomison and Joe Tucci prepared for the Australian Institute of Family Studies, the authors cited a number of studies to illustrate that some teachers use emotional abuse in tandem with other punitive practices to exert control over their students.

Most school districts have long banned corporal punishment from the classrooms in their countries, but the issue of emotional abuse is more difficult to address.

Freda Briggs and Russell Hawkins, in their textbook *Child Protection: A Guide for Teachers and Child Care Professionals*, published in 1996, cited studies that showed young children were often emotionally abused by having their access to toilets overly restricted, by being threatened that their parents would be told of unsatisfactory work or misbehavior, by allowing other children to harass children, by screaming at little ones until they cried, and by labeling students as dumb or stupid.

Some teachers even repeatedly set up their students for failure by giving them tasks that were totally inappropriate for their age and stage of development.

Some children were reportedly pinched, shaken and pulled by their ears. Others had their chairs pulled out from under them.

Some teachers were masterful at executing techniques that filled children with fear and dread. While many of these things could also be classified as physical attacks, the difficulty in proving things, the lack of bruises, and the shame and terror of the victims often allowed the situation to continue unchecked for a considerable time.

A comprehensive outline of the forms of emotional abuse experienced most often in schools was included in a study called "The Emotional Abuse of Our Children: Teachers, schools, and the sanctioned violence of modern institutions."

Written by Dr. Michael Sosteric, it appeared in The Socjournal, a new media journal of sociology and society in 2012.

He described some of the cases of emotional and verbal abuse that can occur in a classroom.

Some teachers use isolation as a means of behavior modification. They move a student from their desk, for example, to a spot on the floor at the front of the classroom, or they make them stand in the corner while other students are permitted to remain at their desks. They can physically move a child's desk beside theirs at the front of the classroom, or just by the doorway, away from all the rest of the group.

This can be emotionally extremely damaging to the student. This is the kind of attention you do not want and it can traumatize a shy youngster for life. Even if your friends support you and you try to make a joke about it, your self-image takes a hit. Keep in mind that our ability to see ourselves with confidence is impacted by how others see us. If they see us as the stupid, ill-behaved one that doesn't fit, that can be the image that is planted in the child's own mind.

Other teachers resort to degrading students to get them to comply. Not only does this pull another piece of the child's self-esteem away, but it also sets up a destructive behavior pattern that they will likely emulate in their own life when they are trying to get control of someone. A child learns a lot more in a classroom than just how to read and write.

Degradation can also be done on the Internet by one group of students against another group of students, as witnessed by the example of the dentistry school students cited at the beginning of this chapter.

Some teachers try to get the upper hand on students by rejecting their presence, by refusing to acknowledge they even exist. The idea is to put the student in his place, to humble them into realizing the classroom doesn't revolve around them.

A teacher's failure to acknowledge a student's presence, instead of enhancing their behavior, cements that they are worthless. It communicates that they deserve to be separated and isolated and ignored. When authority figures isolate you, so do your colleagues. The rejection snowballs into others telling stories about you, pointing fingers at you and laughing at you behind your back. You are treated differently. Instead of moving closer to fitting in and conforming to classroom behaviors, you move farther away until it may not be possible for you to return. Your whole life can change for the worse.

When children are emotionally and verbally abused in school, just as at home, they end up with anger issues, difficulty in forming attachments to others, lose the ability to express empathy and withdraw from the most basic expression of social skills.

Public humiliation is another form of emotional abuse some teachers use to control and manipulate a student. They mock the student in front of others and encourage classmates to join in. You are powerless to walk away: the teacher has made sure you are boxed in using their authority to make you stand and take it. Being shamed in a public place is a form of emotional terror that can cause repercussions to a well-balanced adult. To a young child, who may already be troubled, it is devastating.

The more often teachers use forms of emotional abuse to control children, the more hostile and aggressive the children become. This may manifest itself openly, or quietly with passive-aggressive behavior. The child either becomes extremely unresponsive or becomes overly dependent on their abuser. Their perception of the world around them becomes increasingly negative.

The questions most parents want the answer to is: can this type of emotional abuse still be happening in the modern classroom? The answer is yes.

In chat lines on social media sites you see a parent fuming because her child's teacher said if she didn't do better work, she was in danger of losing her desk privileges and might have to sit on the floor for a week. The child was totally terrified to return to school.

Another parent mention's how his son's name was placed on the blackboard in the classroom under the title "Loser". He was so humiliated he was crying in his room and couldn't eat his supper. When his mother found out the source of his trauma, she called the teacher who seemed unconcerned about it.

Actions such as these can undermine a child's esteem until their long-time creativity and productivity is damaged and they develop social difficulties.

What's to be done about such a situation? What happens when parents discover their children are being humiliated, rejected, isolated or otherwise emotionally abused in their classroom?

Both psychologists and parents have useful strategies.

The first thing parents must do is to understand what emotional abuse is and its ramifications on their child over a long term. This is not a time to tell your child to "tough it out," and just study hard and pass to the next grade where they will get a different teacher. In the months between then and now, irreparable damage may be done to their self-esteem.

In educating yourself about emotional abuse, learn the signs to watch for in your child so that they do not have to suffer in silence. An excellent source of continually upgraded information is the Sanctioned Violence website. (http://sanctionedviolence.sociology.org/)

You must then talk to your child's teacher. Go with an open mind that you will be able to solve this issue together, rather than approaching in a full attack mode.

One parent on a chat line reported how effectively he was able to change the teacher's attitude by recording a conversation he had with his son about what happened at school.

The child cried as he told his father about how ashamed and humiliated he felt for being isolated and made fun of. The child, who has hearing difficulties especially when he had ear infections as was currently the case, told his father he didn't understand what he was supposed to be doing and all of a sudden the teacher was yelling at him and making him move from his desk.

The father called the teacher for a meeting and told her calmly that when his son returned home from class yesterday, he was in a state of distress. This is his version of what happened. The father told the teacher he recorded the interview so that they might both work on a solution to his son's pain together.

He then played the recording. As a preface to that, he advised the teacher that the issue that he was there to discuss was his son's perception of what happened, not whether or not it was true or why it happened. He just wanted to deal with the matter at hand.

By playing the recording and allowing the teacher to see the problem through his son's eyes, the parent and teacher were able to reach an agreement that she would be more emphatic to the child in the future, and would refrain from using such discipline again.

That father asked the teacher what both of them could do, working together, to make the child feel comfortable and safe again in the school environment.

Satisfied with the initial meeting with the teacher, the father nonetheless wrote up a brief, one-page letter to indicate that a meeting was held between himself and the teacher on the specified date about disciplinary tactics in the classroom, and he was assured that the situation would change. He did, however, want to make the principal aware of the situation, should the teacher revert to the behavior that seriously impacted his son's sense of safety and security within the school system. He sent a copy of the letter to the teacher as well.

Should the situation deteriorate further, he has the beginning of a process already in place to insist that changes be made immediately.

You have the right to protect your children and ensure that they are educated without emotional or verbal abuse. If a teacher does not understand that their method of discipline is as harmful as physical discipline, a parent has the right to educate them.

In the rare instance where you might not be able to solve the situation, you should pull your child out of school, obtain legal counsel, and move to the school board or district education office level. Send an email to the teacher, and the principal, to advise them of your action, and tell them they must arrange for the child's lessons to be sent to your home so that they can continue with their studies in a non-abusive environment.

Let both principal and teacher know that the child cannot return to school until the abuse issue has been resolved. If the principal makes inappropriate responses, and threatens you with advocating truancy, for example, encourage them to follow through on their threat so that you will have a chance to publicly defend your point of view. Ask that all correspondence from that point on be forwarded to your lawyer.

Up the stakes and launch a social media campaign, contact local newspapers and television stations and tell them exactly what happened. Furnish them with background information on the perils of long-term verbal and emotional abuse on children. Call on other parents who have heard similar stories to step forward.

Meanwhile, gather as much evidence as you can to support your point of view. Remember the story of two teachers in an Alabama school district who were caught verbally abusing a 10-year-old boy with cerebral palsy.

His mother, suspecting something had gone horribly wrong in the classroom after a child said teachers were being mean to her son, attached a hidden tape recorder to his wheelchair. It captured horrible remarks made by two teachers, who were ultimately suspended on paid leave by the school administration.

Keep in mind that while the vast majority of teachers are well trained and extraordinary in their abilities to uplift children with knowledge and self-esteem, there are always a few bad apples, as in any profession. Do not consider that your child might be lying when they tell stories about bizarre behavior in the classroom.

There are also teachers who have developed mental disorders that have been undetected by their colleagues and supervisors. Whenever a child has a sudden shift in behavior or attitude towards going to school, something has changed and you must investigate. Your child's friends can often be a source of useful information about what is happening in the classroom.

The other way a child may be emotionally or verbally abused at school is outside of the classroom. Bullies can make their life difficult in the schoolyards, in hallways and on the way to and from school if the children walk by themselves. Bullying may be by their colleagues of the same age, or by older children. It may be executed by a pack, or by an individual.

The National Center for Education Statistics (NCES) suggests that about one third of students between the ages of 12 and 18 have been bullied at school. They described bullying as a purposeful attempt by one person to control another through verbal abuse, such as threats or malicious teasing, or exclusion from the group.

In February, 2000, in an article called "Uncovering the hidden causes of bullying and school violence" published in *Counseling and Human Development*, study author Barry Weinhold called bullying the most common type of violence in modern United States society.

Groups who bully together are more often found in high schools and often include aspects of cyberbullying as well as physical confrontation. Individual bullies may deal strictly in emotional and verbal abuse, or they may also resort to physical violence. They are more commonly found at the elementary school level. They can also include an on-line component as well.

Cyber bullies attack their prey in chat rooms or on social network sites, through blogs and website posting or combinations of all of these things. They are emotional bullies, trying to insult and humiliate their victims, gossiping about them or posting private or personal information.

There is one other kind of bully, the social bully, whose goal is to push their victim out of a social group and ostracize them. They ignore or leave out the person from events, and sometimes resort to hiding their personal belongings just to upset them.

In all cases, bullies use insults, name calling, and derogatory remarks as their primary method of communications.

At the school level, sometimes the bullying is linked to racism or religious difference, and at other times it is focused on a student's disabilities or sexual orientation.

The NCES report shows that bullying increases in middle school and emotional bullying is the most prevalent form used. Besides hurling insults and verbal abuse, students will sometimes progress to pushing and spitting on someone. Most of the incidents of bullying occurs within the school. To a lesser extent it happens on school property or buses. Cyberbullying accompanies physical bullying in Grades 6 to 9.

Children who are bullied at school can display long-term impacts, some lasting for life. They have low esteem, problems trusting others and are non-assertive. Others become more aggressive and have anger management issues.

What strategies can schools and communities use to cut out bullying?

One of the most prominent anti-bully programs is OLWEUS, developed by Norwegian professor Dr. Dan Olweus, based on his research that he has conducted since the early 1970s. He was inspired to create the program after three teenagers died in what was believed to be a response to severe bullying from their peers.

In the 1990s, Olweus's ideas about legislation to prohibit bullying were put in place in Norway and Sweden. In the mid-1990s, his Olweus Bully Prevention Program was introduced into the United States, where Olweus partnered with Clemson University in South Carolina professor Dr. Susan P. Limber.

Created particularly for children in Grades 3 to 10, it was aimed at all children, not just bullies. It didn't stop there. It extended to the entire school and into the local community.

Dr. Olweus coined a new definition for bullying. He said a child was being bullied when he is repeatedly exposed to negative actions from one or more persons, and he cannot defend himself.

Examples of bullying included verbal and physical attack, threats, coercion, exclusion, being gossiped about, having personal items taken or damaged and sexual, racial and cyber bullying. What he omitted, however, was bullying by mocking someone through imitating their mannerisms or by stalking.

The program included surveys for students, a school wide guide, a teacher guide, a staff training DVD, the book *Bullying At School*, and two days of training by a certified Olweus trainer. It involved the school principal or vice-principal, a teacher from every grade, a school psychologist or counselor, a nonteaching staff representative, and several parents who are employed with the school district.

Over time, the program became the most emulated and widely used anti-bullying program in the world. Many schools were required by their boards to use the Olweus approach.

But in recent years, flaws have been identified with the program. New approaches are being sought and meanwhile, US President Barack Obama has called bullying an epidemic.

New ways to stem the growth of cyber bullying are also being sought. It is an increasingly serious challenge for today's youth. Cyber bullying occurs when people send messages that threaten or are hurtful to the feelings of other people by means of cell phone messages, emails and social networking sites like Facebook and Twitter. What makes it particularly despicable is that it can be anonymous, and that hikes up the meanness factor. People who are on the receiving end of these messages may start to skip school, experience symptoms of depression, become fearful and mistrustful of others.

Both parents and teachers need to talk about cyber bullying and explain to children why it is wrong and how harmful it can be to those who receive such messages. Children need to develop street smarts about the Internet. They must be told that they cannot trust people they meet online, that they should not give out personal information to strangers online any more than they should get in a stranger's car, and they should never give out their passwords to anyone but their parents.

Most of all, children need to understand from the start that anything they put on the Internet is there forever, and it may come back to haunt them at any time. Children should be told that they should never send a message or put a post on Facebook that they would not want everyone to see.

Parents can also help protect their children from cyber bullying by being mindful of their Internet activities and ensuring that they are safe. Computers for young children should be kept in a high traffic part of the house, instead of in a child's room. Cell phones and computers need to be turned off at night at a certain time, and that rule should be firm.

It is a fine line between allowing your children sufficient privacy and watching what they are doing online. When you feel as a parent that you are not sure what is acceptable, always make the choice in favor of what you honestly feel will keep them safe. That is your foremost responsibility.

Talk to your children about being bullied and if it happens to them, make sure they understand it is not their fault.

If you discover that your child is the target of a cyber-bullying campaign, experts at the National Crime Prevention Council say you must ensure that everything you do from that point forward does not further abuse your child. That means not blaming them for what has happened or swooping in and taking away all their computers and cell phones. In trying to protect them, you must ensure that you do not further victimize them.

Talk to your child about not responding to cyber-bullies. Tell them there is a time to defend themselves, but this is a battle they can't win. If they already have responded, accept that you understand why they did that, but counsel them that should not be their approach in the future.

Document cyber bullying. Move quickly to get your child a new email or phone number.

See if you can get the messages from the cyber bully blocked. Let your child's teacher and principal know this is happening. If you know who the cyber bully is, bring the messages as proof to the school administrators and ask them to contact the parents of the bully.

If they do not respond, contact the police and your website host. People who post inappropriate messages can have their email capability taken from them and be banned from social media sites. The administrators on these sites can sometimes help you locate an anonymous bully.

Police officers in many countries have powers to protect your child from cyber-bullying if threats are involved, or if the inappropriate messages are of a sexual content. If the bully is extorting money or sending messages of hate, these are also against the law in most places. So is continued harassment and cyber-stalking.

Chapter 13: Elder Abuse: How seniors are victims of emotional and verbal abuse

One category of people who are increasingly at risk of emotional and verbal abuse are senior citizens.

The World Health Organization defines elder abuse, or elder mistreatment, as a single act or repeated act, or lack of appropriate action, that occurs in any relationship where there existed an expectation of trust, and which distresses or harms an older person.

The crucial factor revolves around "expectation of trust" that the elderly person has towards their abuser. In most cases the harm is done to them by their spouse, family member, friend or neighbor, people who they believed they could depend on and who would care for them.

Some kinds of elder abuse involve physical acts such as muggings and home break-ins, or even beatings, but the largest category falls under emotional and verbal abuse.

The issue has become a concern all over the world, especially since the World Health Organization made it the focus of an education campaign in 2002. In recent years, concern for how seniors are treated in society has also been expressed by governments and professional groups.

Since 2006 the date June 14 has been designated as World Elder Abuse Awareness Day by the International Network for Prevention of Elder Abuse. A host of events and educational sessions are scheduled each year to coincide with that campaign and raise public awareness that seniors in their lives could be suffering abuse at the hands of those who profess to care for them.

A Crimes Against Older Adults Task Force in the United States defines emotional elder abuse as any verbal or non-verbal act that inflicts emotional pain, anguish or distress on an older adult.

Unlike emotional abuse of children and adults, the emotional abuse of seniors is almost invariably accompanied by other forms of abuse, including physical.

Emotional abuse for seniors often centers on humiliation, threats and degradation. The abuser discovers something that matters to the person and manipulates them by threatening to take away what matters.

The abuser may also ignore the senior.

They may isolate the elderly person from their regular support system of family, friends and group members with whom they previously shared such regular activities as card games or fitness classes.

The abuser may habitually make the senior the scapegoat for anything that goes wrong, and blame them for everything.

The emotional harassment can include insulting or ridiculing the senior and name-calling and cursing. Often the abuser threatens to punish the senior or deprive them of something they find comforting. The senior is the receiver of intimidation.

Sometimes the abuser begins to treat the senior like they are an infant. Other times they will use extreme forms of punishment for so-called misdeeds including confining them to a closet or other dark, poorly-ventilated room, tying them to a chair for long periods of time or screaming at them or terrorizing them in some other way.

Emotional abuse can also involve neglect of seniors by those they trust to look after them. They can be confined, or denied food, clothing, shelter, water, medical care, medicine, items of comfort or safety, and other essentials of care.

Vulnerable seniors can also be abandoned by their caregivers.

Other elements of emotional neglect include refusal to provide emotional support such as love, respect and attention. This manifests itself by the abuser hearing the senior call for help, but ignoring them. In an institution, it involves ignoring the bell calling them to the elder's bedside. It means ignoring their cries for help, or moans.

Emotional abuse also can involve treating the senior coldly and callously.

It can also include neglecting to provide them psychological care such as depression medication or refusing to take them to scheduled therapy sessions.

Caregivers can cut seniors off from the outside world by taking their mail and not delivering it to them, blocking their phone calls, prohibiting them from participating in outside outings and discouraging or stopping visitors from interacting with them.

The abuser won't help the senior do activities that they normally enjoy. They won't even let them watch the television shows they like, read the books they enjoy, or engaging in intellectual activities such as seminars or art shows.

Seniors living in their own homes or in nursing homes can also be subjected to verbal abuse. This includes being yelled at, sworn at, and insulting or mocking. They are the brunt of rude remarks or disdainful observations. They can be criticized and threatened and have their concerns ignored or trivialized.

They are accused of things they didn't do or blamed for whatever goes wrong. Sometimes the senior is subjected to shunning or silence as a form of emotional punishment.

In nursing homes, seniors can be emotionally and verbally abused not just by staff, but also by other residents. Family members and even strangers can also be abusive towards elders.

The Mayo Clinic experts describe the impact of emotional and verbal abuse on seniors as very serious. It can totally destroy their quality of life. The increased stress can trigger depression and dementia and an increased sense of helplessness.

It can contribute to the senior experiencing a decline in their functional abilities and make them more dependent on their abuser. The result is a heightened psychological decline and in some cases, premature death.

Seniors who are victimized with emotional and verbal abuse are three times more likely to die than those who are not abused. Those who live can have lasting psychological damage.

Being abused can impact the seniors' ability to eat properly and they may suffer the effects of malnutrition.

Many seniors are emotionally fragile when they have to leave their long-time home and enter an institution, and this makes them especially vulnerable to the abuser. There are cases where the added stress of being emotionally and verbally abused is so pervasive that their immune systems are weakened and they succumb to stress-related illnesses.

The Center for Problem-Oriented Policing says in their Problem Guide on Elderly Abuse that not only do the vulnerable seniors suffer, but also their families and communities. The victims often lose trust in their caregivers, the institutions in which they live and the system that has failed them in their most vulnerable time. They also lose trust in those they believed would care for them in their old age.

Some older victims of emotional abuse blame themselves for what is happening to them. They are conscious of being a burden on their caregivers. If their own children are the abusers, they are even more ashamed that they are responsible for raising a person who acts this way.

When one senior is aware of a senior friend being emotionally or verbally abused, they suffer with them and often feel powerless to help.

According to the Administration on Aging, a branch of the Administration for Community Living, US Department of Health and Human Services, abuse of the elderly is particularly reprehensible since most of the victims are frail and vulnerable and unable to escape. They are depending on people they trust to meet basic needs in life, and when they are abused, the impact is so devastating some never recover.

As with all kinds of emotional and verbal abusers, those who prey on the elderly may be either men or women, family members or caregivers, or even friends.

While the issue of elder abuse encompasses a number of different kinds of abuses, including physical, sexual and neglect, in this chapter the focus is on emotional and verbal abuse.

Manifestations of emotional abuse include, besides threats and humiliation, exploitation. Trusted caregivers may misuse or take funds or assets from a senior.

They also inflict mental pain on the elderly person, causing them anguish and distress. Verbal abuse includes intimidations and threats.

Sometimes the abuse a senior receives from their tormentor is so severe that the elder falls into a form of self-neglect, their spirit broken, and they stop caring for themselves and looking after their own basic needs.

How can elder emotional and verbal abuse be recognized?

Sometimes it is difficult to pick up because the victim is afraid to talk about it for fear that it will get worse. Sometimes the senior has a mistrust of the police or other authority figures and is afraid to talk to them. Some are embarrassed or feeling that complaining with be futile. Estimates are that less than a third of seriously abused seniors actually complain to the police.

There is no one clear indication of emotional or verbal abuse but rather a number of signals. Seniors who begin to withdraw from activities they once enjoyed send a signal that something in their life or health has changed. So does a change in their normal level of alertness as well as signs of feeling depressed.

A sudden change in their financial situation can be a red flag that they are being emotionally and financially exploited.

If caregivers witness exchanges between the senior and their spouse that includes belittling, threats and other exercises of control, they should be conscious that this may be a pattern of emotional abuse.

Another signal is an obviously strained relationship between the senior and their spouse, caregiver or another family member. Frequent arguments between that person and the senior, signs of fear or distaste on the face of the senior, and disrespectful attitudes are clues something is wrong.

Keep in mind that many seniors suffer psychological abuse in silence, fearful that the price of speaking out will be too high. Ask insightful questions and notice little exchanges between the seniors and those responsible for their well-being.

You do not have to be able to solve the problem. You just have to pass on your concerns to those who can do something about it.

As with all victims of emotional and verbal abuse, seniors suffer from low self-esteem. They may also have mood swings, be unable to look directly at people and make eye-contact, express shyness to speak or show signs of sustained anger.

They may give off a sense of hopelessness or appear fearful.

One of the most in-depth looks at the issue of elder abuse became public in 1998 when the Administration on Aging and the Administration for Children and Families released a National Elder Abuse Incidence Study.

Requested by U.S. Congress, the study was conducted by the National Center for Elder Abuse at the American Public Human Services Association (formerly the American Public Welfare Association) in collaboration with Westat, Inc., a Maryland-based social science and research firm.

The shocking truth the study revealed is that reported incidents of elder abuse represent only the "tip of the iceberg". Study authors estimated at least half a million seniors in the US alone sustain some kind of abuse. For every one case that is reported and dealt with, five more are happening behind closed doors.

In the United Kingdom, a Prevalence Study into the extent of elder abuse in their communities conducted for the Action on Elder Abuse organization concluded about 342,000 seniors experience some abuse in their own homes.

In Australia, it is estimated that about three per cent of people over the age of 65 have suffered abuse in some form. However, the New South Wales (NSW) on Abuse of Older People puts the figure as high as five per cent. A further eight percent of people reported they knew some senior who had been victimized by abuse.

The problem is expected to grow with a worldwide aging demographic. In the United States alone, going back to the incidence study, there are about 44 million people over 60. But even as public interest in improving the lives of seniors increases, the emotional and verbal abuse of elders has been largely unaddressed.

However, some details of the problem did come to light through the research associated with The National Elder Abuse Incidence Study. They learned that female seniors are abused more than males, seniors over the age of 80 are abused more than younger seniors, and in almost 90 percent of the cases of abuse, the senior knows their abuser.

Most of the time their abusers are family members, and two-thirds of those are adult children or spouses. Other potential abusers are friends and neighbors, volunteer workers, paid care workers, and solicitors.

Adult children and relatives with sustain substance abuse issues are particularly prone to abuse. One study identified potential elder abusers as being more likely chronically unemployed and dependent on the older person.

The element that exists in almost all reported cases is that the abuser is in a position of trust. Some seniors are courted with charm and thoughtful gestures by their abusers, and once they allow them to move into their homes or rely on them, the emotional and verbal abuse starts.

Health authorities refer to these relationships as the abuser "grooming" the senior and then taking control over them.

Seniors most vulnerable to grooming are those with no spouse and no adult children regularly checking on them. Many of these abusers are looking to obtain the elderly person's money and estate.

In the case where one spouse verbally and emotionally abused the other all through their younger years, this usually continue as they both grow old. Statistically it is referred to as "domestic violence grown old".

Sometimes abuse flares up when an older couple, both frail, try to care for each other but lack the resources and stamina to do it. Care turns to anger and pettiness.

For seniors who live outside of their homes, such as in nursing homes or special care facilities, abuse can come from controlling care-givers in the form of taunting and teasing, withholding of comforts and slowness in providing care for incontinence issues.

Sometimes the verbal abuse that includes insensitivity to the elderly person's religious or personal beliefs comes from care-givers who have insufficient training or resources to handle certain situations.

In rare cases, the abuse may be done unwittingly by a care-giver following a policy or process that is ill-considered. This abuse, upon investigation, is tagged "poor practice" and can be fixed with a change in management directives or a change in management.

There are other triggers for people to target seniors for abuse.

The burden of caring for senior parents or relatives on people who are already stretched thin by life's demands can make them impatient in providing care, and that impatience can quickly turn into abuse. It starts with threats and the trivializing of the senior's concerns and progresses to verbal abuse. They tell the senior they are eating too slowly and the food will be taken from them if they can't eat faster. They may even be threatened with force feeding.

Sometimes the senior's caregiver becomes abusive from frustration. Trying to care for an adult who has dementia or Alzheimer's disease can expose a caregiver to aggression and nastiness, and, unable to distinguish the behavior from the illness, they lash out with shouting and nastiness. One fourth of abusers who are caregivers admit that their emotional abuse followed their own victimization by the senior. Statistics show that seniors with Alzheimer's disease are twice as likely to be abused as those who do not have the disease.

The burden of care can also cause some family members caring for seniors to become abusive. They may be stressed financially, emotionally and physically to provide the care and their patience is stretched thin. Suffering from burn-out, aggressive thoughts and conflicted motivations themselves, they lash out verbally at the slightest provocation.

The NEAIS study warns that elder abuse will increase as the population ages if steps are not taken now to address it.

Certain types of seniors are more apt to be victims of emotional and verbal abusers than others. Those most at risk experience memory problems or physical disabilities, especially those who are completely unable to care for themselves.

Depression, lack of social support, and loneliness also make seniors more vulnerable to be targets of an abuser, as does a senior's abuse of alcohol or other substances.

Seniors who must end their years in shared living situations are also more likely to be abused.

What are the characteristics most commonly found in the person who abuses elderly people?

The study identified specific common character traits in care-givers who verbally and emotionally abuse. These include workers who feel overwhelmed with their workload and are resentful that caring for the elderly is what they have to do for a living.

Many of them will have a history of being abused as both children and adults or they are abusive parents or spouses. Some have mental health issues or are caring for a family member because they are unemployed. If they live with the senior they care for, the possibility for abuse is higher.

In some cases, seniors are abused verbally and emotionally by more than one person. Two family members may team up and upset the elderly person with threats of putting them on the street or turning them out to an institution. In rare cases, both a child and a grandchild can team up for the abuse.

Overall, the psychological abuse of seniors is even tougher to detect than child abuse, largely because of the social isolation of the elderly. They do not have to go out of their home every day to school or to work. They can be forgotten and ignored much easier.

There are also conflicting perceptions and difficulty in pinning down the problem. For example, the Center for Problem-Oriented Policing reported on a survey of nursing assistants from 10 nursing homes participating in an abuse prevention training program found that half of them admitted to yelling at a patient in the past 30 days. Larger facilities seem to have a higher rate of complaints, as do for-profit facilities.

The Center noted that while it has been suggested that seniors living in nursing homes are more at risk of emotional and physical abuse, about 90 percent of cases reported to adult protective services occur in domestic settings.

In long-term care facilities, emotional and physical abuse is most commonly committed by nurse's assistants. They are the ones who have more contact with the seniors than other staffers. Another factor may that they have less education than nurses and doctors and other health care professionals.

What is being done to address the problem?

People who suspect a senior is being emotionally abused are encouraged to report their concerns to appropriate authorities. Once a complaint is filed, in most countries there is a process for follow-up assessments. The assessor will check on how the senior is cared for day to day, their activities and their social interactions. In an effort to get a clear view of the subject, the assessor may ask the senior who they like to spend time with and why.

If the complaint pertains to a senior who is a resident in a nursing home, the assessor will discuss how the senior is normally spoken to by the staff, including what they are called. They will be asked how often they have visitors, are taken on outings, and receive mail.

If emotional abuse is detected, the senior is immediately moved to a safe place. They will be assigned a counselor and if necessary, medication to calm them temporarily and help them sleep safely.

Treatment for the emotionally abused senior also includes scheduling follow-up visits with the victim and often a follow-up with the abuser with appropriate corrective steps taken. Educational rehabilitation may be ordered or, depending on the severity of the abuse, criminal action.

Family members who are planning to place a senior in a nursing home should tour the nursing home and interview the care team before placing a loved one in their care. Families need to keep regular checks on the senior and ask to be kept aware of any changes in their behavior.

Nursing homes, hospitals and seniors' homes can be responsive to the issue by putting protocols in place to handle complaints and investigations. Supervisory staff need to keep a close eye on senior patients and be educated on how to detect signs of emotional or verbal abuse.

Physicians, dentists, hairstylists and others who help look after seniors may also be in a position to detect problems. Comprehensive education programs for them as well as nurses and other health care workers should focus on observing the signs of abuse and neglect and a clear process on what to do if it is observed.

Bankers should also be educated to recognize incidents of financial exploitation and to have protocols in place to ensure that seniors making significant changes in their financial matters are properly counseled.

Chapter 14: What Happens When the Emotional Abuser is Unstable?

One of the most difficult and dangerous forms of emotional and verbal abuse occurs when the abuser has serious mental disorders. They may be a narcissist, a sociopath, a psychopath or just a toxic person.

They do not play their malicious games by anyone else's rules. Strategies that can be effective in dealing with other emotional abusers can be useless in reaching these severely disturbed people.

Initiatives that might ignite changes in other people can be seized by these serial abusers and turned and twisted back on the victim to cause unimaginable pain.

In this chapter, we will look at each of these specific abusers and how they impact their victims.

The narcissist, whose every action centers on the pursuit of their own gratification fueled by their egotistic admiration of their own attributes, is a master at control as a form of emotional and verbal abuse.

Because they believe they are smarter and more capable than everyone around them, their nature is that they must control all the other, dumber people. They will use any means to accomplish their goal, but emotional and verbal abuse are common weapons.

Their emotional terror goes further than a regular abuser, however, and enters the realm of what psychologists refer to as mental abuse. In lay person's terms, the narcissist is capable of making someone crazy. To cover their own guilt, they are adept at making their spouse, sibling or child feel that they are "crazy".

They can do tremendous harm to their victims and some may never recover. They create a climate in which their victim starts to believe that they are reacting in an overly-emotional or irrational way. They are adept at drawing other people into the web to the point that the victim's family, neighbors and even co-workers seriously start to believe that they have become unbalanced, when all the while it is the narcissist who is irrational and unbalanced.

It is a devious form of emotional abuse that the narcissist perfects in an effort to gain attention and sympathy and to cover his or her own terrible behavior. The narcissist is never to blame for anything that goes wrong. It is always someone else at fault, and that person is most likely the one who lives with them.

The narcissist preys on their partner's emotion and skillfully adds so much stress and confusion that they can take full control of their mental processes. If the narcissist's victim arrives home in a good mood, for example, the narcissist will become extremely angry. If the victim is angry or upset, the narcissist will make a show of ignoring them. If the victim is hurt, suffering or in any way vulnerable, the narcissist will move with powerful aggression to destroy them further and make them feel even worse. They are nasty in the extreme.

The narcissist, however, expects his or her partner to drop everything and rush to rescue them from their own emotional ups and downs. If the narcissist feels angry about something that happened outside of the home, they will turn their anger on their partner and insist that they perform acts of humiliation as a kind of punishment because the world has upset the narcissist. If the narcissist becomes upset, they expect their partner to put their own life on hold and put all their efforts into soothing the narcissist and making them feel better.

Some of the other emotional abuse techniques wielded by the narcissist include withholding love and affection and even intimacy, dismissing all opinions or points of view expressed by their partner, demeaning their partner by telling them they are stupid and their thoughts are insignificant and dumb, changing the subject abruptly and halting any conversation that challenges them in any way, and constantly accusing their victim of offenses they haven't committed.

A common accusation is that they are seeing someone else behind the narcissist's back or that they are spending money on themselves at the detriment of the family, or even that they deliberately cooked something that upset the narcissist's stomach.

They judge and criticize. They seize control over the clothes that their partner buys and wears. They determine whether a partner should have long or short hair.

As soon as the narcissist senses something is important to their victim, they trivialize it.

If their victim attempts to live their own life or achieve any degree of independence by taking a course or learning a skill or even advancing on the job, the narcissist will undermine them and threaten them from accepting any advancement. If they do not do this with aggression, they will do it with manipulation to convince the person that they do not want to advance.

The narcissist threatens divorce, threatens to leave their victim penniless, threatens to take the children in the dead of night and run off. They threaten hurtful actions against people the victim loves.

The narcissist, who is conscious of everything, pretends to forget significant things as a means of undermining the victim's reality. They will say they didn't know or weren't told something important and blame the victim.

Often the narcissist will make their partner a slave or treat them as a child who must be totally controlled for their own good. They unleash tirades of anger that can quickly turn to physical abuse.

Getting help as the victim of a narcissist's emotional and verbal abuse can be difficult, because the abuser is often an outstanding member of the community and may hold an important job. They can be lawyers, doctors, ministers or even politicians.

Because outsiders hold the narcissist in great respect, unable to see their true nature, the suffering spouse starts to wonder what is wrong with them and if they really are unstable, crazy, or losing their minds.

The narcissist is able to damage the victim so grievously because they know them well and understand what they value, what they love, and what they want to achieve. Once they attack and crumble the foundations of the person, it becomes impossible for them to recreate their own self-esteem.

A long-time relationship with a narcissist can utterly destroy a person's sense of self.

What can be done to save the victim?

Even if the victim is aware that the abuser is a narcissist or suffers from Narcissistic Personality Disorder, the reality is that they are no more and no less than a serious psychological abuser. This is a situation where "sticking it out" will not make it any better; in fact the abuse will continue to get worse. Ultimately, there can be serious impact on the victim's cognitive skills.

Leaving is the best option when it comes to dealing with a narcissist, advises Dr. Diane England, who has written extensively on issues of abuse and post traumatic stress disorder relationships. The price of staying is too high, counsels England, who is also the author of *The Post Traumatic Stress Disorder Relationship*.

If living with a narcissist sounds terrifying, it is. But if it is possible to be in an even worse situation, it is to be married to or living with a sociopath.

A sociopath is a person suffering from antisocial personality disorder. It is impossible for them to have any kind of a normal relationship largely because they lack the capacity to experience even the slightest degree of empathy. Their world is all about them, not others.

The trouble is, you do not know how damaged they are until you are caught in their web.

In the beginning the sociopath is the perfect boyfriend or girlfriend. They are also the biggest liar you will ever meet and a kind of chameleon, absorbing all the pictures in your mind of the perfect mate and becoming it.

It is only after the relationship progresses that the sociopath's behavior changes dramatically and terrifyingly. The partner then becomes like a tortured spider in their web, and the level of emotional and verbal abuse escalates to an alarming level. To the sociopath, the relationship is all a game; to the victim, it can mean being damned to their own private hell. The sociopath finds ways to isolate their victim from everyone and make them a captive.

During the dating game, the sociopath is fun and charismatic, seducing friends of his or her prey and convincing everyone that a perfect match is unfolding before them. Things couldn't be better.

But once the couple moves in together or marries, the sociopath assumes total control of the victim and isolates them from everyone. The sociopath is jealous of anyone who is in any way connected to their prey. The victim becomes a possession.

The emotional abuse starts with the sociopath making demeaning comments about the victim's friends and accuses them of serious character flaws and sets up ways that they appear in a bad light. The victim, not wanting their new perfect partner to think there is anything wrong with them, begins to disengage from friends.

First the sociopath tells them, for example, that their friends are all alcoholics. When the victim doesn't disengage quickly enough, the follow-up suggestion is that the victim is an alcoholic.

The victim is very upset, being conscious that the accusation is not true. Determined to prove the perfect partner wrong, the victim stays further away from the friends and begins to focus their entire life on their mate.

The emotional abuse, subtle by insidious grows and the sociopath moves into the gaming mode. In an effort to please them, the victim slowly starts to surrender their own identity and stops considering themselves at all.

In Martha Stout's book *The Sociopath Next Door*, it is clear that the sociopath will stay at his game until his prey is totally destroyed. The sociopath has no moral anchor, no sense of being part of a society. To them, other people are nothing but objects.

Sociopaths destroy people because of their own underlying rage and resentment, even though they may ooze charm. They are incapable of having real feelings as others know them.

What can be done to assist the person who gets involved in a relationship with a sociopath?

They have to leave as quickly as possible, or they will be totally emotionally destroyed. You will have no life of your own. Things will not change for the better, ever. They will just get darker and darker.

When you leave a sociopath, make no effort to stay as "friends" or strive for an amiable separation. Sever all contact. It is the only hope for survival. Otherwise, he will continue to punish you until there is nothing of the person who used to be you remaining.

Keep in mind that the sociopath can be physically abusive and can also be extremely destructive. You cannot let them back in your life ever again. Ensure that you have help and a safe place to stay when you leave.

The best that you can hope for is that the sociopath, following a typical behavior stereotype, will conclude that you are no longer useful and will turn their attentions to charming a replacement.

Counselors who have experience treating victims who were emotionally and verbally abused by sociopaths report that in some cases, the victim is not consciously aware that they were suffering abuse. They know that they feel bad about themselves and have no self-esteem, but they do not know how that happened or why it happened.

Another horrifying emotional abuser is the psychopath. Their psychological abuse is usually wrapped up in physical and economic abuse as well. In extreme cases, they can push their victims to take their own lives.

Their emotional abuse swings like an up and down pendulum. One minute they acknowledge the worth of their victim; the next minute they devalue it and destroy the victim with hurtful comments.

Psychopaths are capable of killing their victims or inflicting so much psychological, physical and financial abuse on them that they drive their victims to kill themselves.

Demeaning, abusing and killing are what psychopaths do; it makes them feel good. They have no empathy for their victims, and no conscience, so no act is unthinkable.

Sometimes they are extremely clever and are able to bully their way to the top of corporations or institutions or even governments. They want to inflict damage and will act in any way to accomplish that. At the crux of their behavior is a need to have power and control over everyone.

We have looked at narcissists, sociopaths and psychopaths. There is one more group prone to emotional abuse and that is what has been loosely labeled as the "toxic people" group.

Just as physical toxins in the environment harm people's physical health, toxic people are detrimental to their mental health. Emotional and verbal abuse are their weapons of choice.

Relationships or even casual encounters with toxic people throughout our lives can leave long-term effects on our emotional health. Toxic people are well-versed in emotional abuse and know just how to assess the weakness of their prey and the ways they can be taken advantage of.

Toxic people are the takers in this world. They are the vicious gossips, the unrelenting complainers who could try the patience of a saint. They are constantly putting others down and making them feel guilty. They manipulate people to meet their needs, but are unavailable when others need their support. In fact, when people most need them, they are emotionally cruel.

They start arguments and ignite conflict wherever they go. They create drama and they love it.

When they are challenged on the lies and gossips they spread, they deny that they made the hurtful remarks.

Toxic people withhold key information so that others will suffer or struggle needlessly. They refuse to communicate and withdraw emotionally from their intimate partner. They regularly resort to the silent treatment.

The abuser believes that their viewpoint is the only one that matters, that their feelings are the only ones that count and their perception of things is accurate. Their insistence on their position can cause those living with them to start doubting themselves.

The toxic person wants to control the actions of everyone around them. They insist on having their own way and will threaten, lie, cheat and manipulate to achieve that.

Toxic abusers are adept at emotional blackmail. They extract information from their victims and then use it against them to control them.

In an intimate relationship, they are the partner who keeps threatening to leave, rejects their partner repeatedly, and uses fear tactics to maintain control. If the abused partner expresses hurt at the toxic person's behavior, their feelings are dismissed as invalid.

Toxic people experience drastic mood changes and dramatic emotional outbursts. They take one position one day, and a completely opposite one the next. This creates emotional abuse against anyone living with them since it leaves them in a state of confusion and doubt. They are always wondering where they stand and what will become next. This creates a climate of anxiety and stress.

Toxic people often resort to verbal abuse as well, expressing their mood swings with screaming, threatening, and excessive blaming. They belittle their partners, call them names and criticize them. They make fun of their partners in public, damaging their sense of self-worth.

People who were emotionally abused as children are more apt to stay in a relationship with a toxic person. They are used to being with a controlling person and it triggers a certain familiarity, even though it is a destructive situation.

The toxic person who is the abuser may also have been abused as a child, but took a different road. They learned how to be manipulative and emotionally abusive to achieve power. In their own way, they are likely struggling with feelings of powerlessness and anger. They are attracted to people they perceive as weaker than themselves.

When it comes to leaving the toxic person who is abusing you, it helps to understand why you were attracted to that kind of person in the first place, and what deep need within you they might have been meeting. That is the first step to restoring your self-worth and finding the courage to get the toxic person out of your life.

Fortunately, avoiding toxic people is generally easier than avoiding narcissists, sociopaths and psychopaths.

The best strategy is just to walk away if you are in a crowd where a toxic person is holding court with malicious gossip. You cannot win an argument with such a person. It is better to express your disinterest or disagreement with a quiet gesture of moving out of their range.

The emotional abuse of the toxic person is a roaming target and not always directed right at you. In the case of gossip, it can land on anyone who will listen.

However, sometimes you are caught in the crossfire of abuse from such a person because a conflict has occurred and they want to drive you to the ground. You may have made an innocent mistake, or they may be falsely accusing you of something you didn't do.

Either way, a good strategy is to again remove yourself from the situation. You cannot win because the toxic person does not want a calm explanation; they want to heap verbal abuse in a public show first. If you move away, they either have to resort to physically grabbing you, a calculated risk on their part, or they have to shout after you that the disagreement isn't over. Perhaps it is not, but it is for that moment.

The important part of handling the toxic person is to avoid being roped into stooping to their level and countering their verbal and emotional assaults. If you must engage in conversation when they challenge you, state the facts calmly and firmly and then stop talking. Let it go; you can never win this war.

Toxic people can be seen in retail outlets harassing sales personnel or customer service staff. They are the person shouting at the airport reservations staff, or the loud voice demanding better service in doctor's offices or at nursing stations.

When a toxic person starts verbally abusing you in a public place, it helps to remember that others will be more sympathetic to the person who is taking the abuse than to the person who is delivering it. Few people want to witness tirades delivered to others in public. It is uncomfortable for all concerned.

If the toxic person is someone who shows up regularly in your life, like a co-worker or a family member, you still need to stop them from impacting your life in a detrimental way. Do not allow them to use you or make you feel guilty when you have to say no.

If a toxic person is in your life and emotionally and verbally abusing you, you have to remove them from your life. If the person is a friend, you must distance yourself. If they are a family member, limit your encounters.

Chapter 15: Why We Can't Just Turn the Other Cheek as a Society

The emotional and verbal abuse of seniors is a problem broader than just the victim and the perpetrator. Its roots go deep into our culture and extend into our institutions, our educational and health systems, and our criminal justice system.

According to the Center for Problem-Oriented Policing, cultural factors can contribute to emotional abuse.

For example, cultures that show less respect for the value of seniors tend to create a value system that promotes more abuse towards them and behaviors that devalue their contribution to society. Discrimination against the aged in a society is linked with increased abuse.

However, cultures that place high value on each person's willingness to help others tend to have less emotional and verbal abuse overall. On the other hand, in many societies where profit is valued over people, a climate of abuse towards those who are not considered as useful as others can foster abusive behaviors.

Cultures that worship power and wealth, winning, and the use of violence to solve conflict, perhaps unintentionally create societies where the strong have a tendency to take advantage of the weak.

More and more psychologists are turning to culture to explain the increase of bullying behavior. Researchers have signaled out such institutions as the World Wrestling Federation (WWF) as a means of praising bullying behavior for entertainment's sake.

Corporate cultures that foster managers who are forgiven for any kind of behavioral transgressions as long as the bottom line looks good have been blamed for escalating psychological abuse in the workplace. When institutions do not have a zero-tolerance policy against bullying, and the strength and manpower to enforce it, they promote worker abuse by their neglect. If people are not reminded to function with civility towards each other, then bullying becomes a standard and is sometimes even praised as an expression of power, aggression and the winning spirit.

A mass media in developed countries that consistently recognizes more prominently deviant and negative behavior as opposed to consistent and kind behavior is a daily reminder to attention seekers of what works. Acting outrageously makes headlines; acting with decorum and civility does not.

In earlier chapters the work of Dr. Olweus and his anti-bullying program was discussed. Some of his research indicated a high success rate for his program in his native Scandinavian countries, while the figures did not always come out the same in the United States.

Researchers now believe that culture was the defining factor in the different outcomes.

Scandinavian companies have a reputation for respecting social justice and Norway in particular has one of the lowest crime rates and highest standards of living in the world. It is a culture that fosters the growth of the underdog. Neighboring Sweden advocates for world harmony through the Nobel Peace Prize program.

Even prisoners are treated like normal people with acceptable behaviors because of the belief that is what they will turn into. Sentences are limited to 21 years to allow for the person to return to a normal life. The rate of Norwegian criminals returning to a life of crime after incarceration is considerably lower than that of the United States.

Abuse is particularly high in countries that present harsh punishments as the answer to solving serious social problems. Even the threat of punishment is used daily to keep people in line. There are mountains of laws dictating what is acceptable behavior, but still people who ignore them. The United States has one of the highest rates of incarceration of its criminals and the culture is that the prisons should certainly not have a country club atmosphere.

Even children are raised with a strong emphasis on behaving properly or suffering punishment. This idea of "be good or else" starts at home, but it is reinforced in educational institutions and community organizations. At the basis of all parenting decisions is an inherent belief that what makes a child good is the punishment they receive when they are bad.

Many people in positions of power over children believe that the way to stop bullying is to firmly tackle the bullying child and stop them from getting away with it. Again, there is the understanding that if the act of bullying is punished with more bullying by the parent or authority figure, the problem will right itself.

If schools do not punish bullies with threats and suspensions, parents seek redress in the court system. They want to see the bully suffer. If school administrators won't do that and make it obvious, then we want to see the school administrator suffer.

There is a school of thought that America and many other developed countries have created some of their own problems of emotional and verbal abuse by promoting punishment as the solution to eradicating the country's most serious social problems.

It may be time to re-examine how culture impacts on the growing issues of emotional and verbal abuse and see if by re-adjusting our collective thinking, we might be able to make societal changes.

In the Olweus Bullying Prevention Program, for example, there is a part where it is suggested school staff meet regularly to discuss their approach to eradicating bullying, and to discuss what seems to be working and what is not working. Evaluation of each approach is stressed.

Each school has the potential to implement the program in their own way, but for most, there is little variation on the theme of punishment for bullying behavior and supervision to stop it in progress. This is in contrast to Norway, where most schools use the same program, but promote a more gentle approach to bullies, encouraging the offenders to be aware that they are capable of better behavior.

Olweus is one expert who sees treatment of bullying solely through punishment is a futile effort. Children who bully others and who then get caught and punished often return to their bullying behavior with a vengeance. They want to "get even" with the victim who exposed them. Instead of being encouraged to become a better person, subtly they are instead nudged into revenge and more abusive behavior.

Cultural factors that impact emotional and verbal abuse also include poverty and lack of education into what good parenting skills involve.

One of the most powerful ways that culture impacts behavior is through how we communicate our feelings and what acceptable behavior is. If you feel joyful but you join into a conversation where everyone else is sad, you immediately alter your tone and start saying sad things too.

If a group of parents are talking about how they threatened a child within an inch of his life to buckle down and start studying, you begin to think that threats are a way to enforce productive behavior.

A research project into how communication impacts how we think was conducted by Igor Grossmann, Phoebe Ellsworth and Ying-Yi Hong and the results were published in the peer-reviewed *Journal of Experimental Psychology* (February, 2012).

Their theory was that culture impacted the way people pay attention to emotional information in the environment and they set out to prove it.

They used as a foundation for their study the observation that negative feelings stereotypically are reflected in the Russian culture. They noted that Russians will often admit that they focus more on negative feelings than their counterparts in the United States do.

In the first study, groups of American and Russian college students were asked to look at a series of pictures. Some were just pictures of clouds. They were neither happy nor sad images. Other pictures were of happy scenes, and still others were of sad scenes.

The students studied the images one after another on their computer screens.

They were told that this was part of memory test that would follow. The American students looked longest at the positive pictures and spent less on the neutral ones and negative ones. The Russian students, however, spent longer viewing the negative pictures than the positive or neutral ones.

The researchers pressed on to give their theory another test. They decided to manipulate cultures and see what happened.

In the second study, the students selected were all Russian Latvians. Significantly, the Latvian culture is more closely aligned to European cultural influences than the Russian culture. The people are bicultural, meaning overall they tend to show the influence of both cultures.

This time the students were shown strings of letters (such as BRANE) and asked if the letters made a word. They pressed one button if it was a word and one button if it was not. In the instance of BRANE for example, the answer was not.

The strings of letters that were actual words were Latvian adjectives that were either negatives, such as lazy, or positive, such as friendly.

Before being shown the letters, however, the participants saw pictures that either depicted symbols of Latvian culture, symbols of Russian culture, or neutral pictures.

When the students saw the Latvian cultural symbols, they responded faster to the positive words than the negative ones. When the same students saw Russian symbols, they responded more quickly to the negative words than to the positive one.

This solidified the earlier conclusion that the Russian culture contributes to people paying more attention to negative information than positive.

When applied to the issue of the impact of culture on emotional and verbal abuse, the impact is interesting. It suggests that the culture in which we live affects our attitude by impacting what we pay attention to in our world.

If you live in a culture that looks at issues positively, you will be in a lighter mood than if your culture pushes you to take more of an interest in negative things, which then leads to moods of sadness and depression.

So if in your culture good behavior, a positive, is believed to stem from other good behavior, you may impact attitudes towards parenting and learning that are quite different than if you believe that good behavior stems from negative behavior, as in punishment or abuse.

Conclusion

By examining the causes and effects of emotional and verbal abuse on children and adults in a variety of different settings and environments, we can summarize that the causes are varied and could not be contained in one single explanation.

We have also discovered that in many cases, there are a multitude of factors in play, from the abuser's personal history, to substance abuse, to the mental health of the abuser.

Nonetheless, we are able to assess the likelihood of abuse aimed at certain most vulnerable people in society and to a certain extent, to identify characteristics standard in abusers.

We have also studied the impact of abuse on individuals and society in general, and the complex approaches to dealing with this serious social issue.

We are keenly aware that the issue is not going to right itself and go away. Instead, particularly with elder emotional abuse as the population ages, it may be even worse.

We close this examination and analysis of the subject with a keen understanding that behaviors that create hardship and pain for the weakest and most vulnerable members of our society must be modified so that the dignity and respect of each person is protected.

This will take more research, more resources and perhaps a complete change of societal attitudes if firm action is to be considered.

There is one additional form of emotional and verbal abuse that has not been addressed in this book because it does not fit within the predominant categories being discussed.

But it is worthy of discussion as we prepare to wrap up the analysis.

The rarer form of psychological abuse being discussed is the Stockholm syndrome.

It is a term used to describe a strange and paradoxical relationship that can develop between an abuser and a victim when one is a kidnapper and the other is a hostage.

When a person is first kidnapped, they live in terror of their kidnapper. They have been pulled out of their normal life and their regular environment and deprived of the company of those they love and the regular comforts of their lives. Their stress can bring them to the breaking point.

In such a vulnerable state, they desperately reach for even the smallest perceived kindness from their abuser. They hope that one small kindness might lead to another and even special treatment where the terror would lessen a little.

This desperate need they develop for care and comfort leaves them totally in the control of their kidnapper and the hope of special treatment. In their moments of extreme weakness and vulnerability, they bond to the strength and power of their kidnappers. They want their keeper to know they are lovable and in return, they fall in love with their abusers even while they simultaneously hate and fear them.

Abused men and women who for whatever circumstances are forced to stay in long-term relationships with their abusers can develop a kind of Stockholm syndrome as well. Though their freedom has been taken from them, as well as kindness and comfort and affection and all the things that help people to thrive, they stay on in some psychological limbo of being in love and hate at the same time.

In recent years, more research is being directed at why the abused person stays with their abuser in intimate relationships, and this reality is increasingly seen as an explanation.

The techniques of intermittent reinforcement provide a reasonable explanation for the bizarre love dependence that can develop in psychologically abusive situations.

Because the abuser reinforces a behavior, emotion or attitude on an unpredictable timetable, the victim snatches at the crumbs of occasional rewards and tries endlessly to create the circumstances that will repeat them.

The traumatized victim is somehow able to deny the horror of day to day life and places all hopes for a safe and caring protector onto the abuser. Cognitive behavior specialists suggest that this strange relationship develops when the victim starts to repress the abuse they are receiving and thus their urge to escape.

The occasional positive experience with their abuser strengthens their illusion that things will get better soon.

Psychologists have learned a great deal about emotional and verbal abuse and in recent years, the number of scientific studies focused in this area has increased. Through continued study, we will be further enlightened about these complex human behaviors and will hopefully be able to determine a means of protecting the dignity and respect of each person, regardless of age or vulnerability.

Other books available by author on Kindle, paperback and audio

Are You A Narcissist? The Ultimate Guide to Finding Out If You Suffer From Narcissism and the Narcissistic Personality Disorder

CPSIA information can be obtained at www.ICGtesting.com
Printed in the USA
BVOW02s0323261015

424131BV00001BA/7/P